D1138411

et One Vagabond Poet One Vaga

Series editor: Colin Waters

Be the First to Like This: New Scottish Poetry

Edited by
Colin Waters

Vagabond Voices
Glasgow

© AA.VV as listed in the contents 2014

First published in September 2014 by
Vagabond Voices Publishing Ltd.,
Glasgow,
Scotland.

ISBN 978-1-908251-35-0

The authors' rights to be identified as authors of this book under the
Copyright, Designs and Patents Act 1988 have been asserted.

Printed and bound in Poland

Cover design by Mark Mechan

Typeset by Park Productions

The publisher acknowledges subsidy towards
this publication from Creative Scotland

For further information on Vagabond Voices, see the website,
www.vagabondvoices.co.uk

To the Scottish Poetry Library and all who sail in her

Contents

Foreword
by Liz Lochhead

I remember just over forty years ago taking part in an event called Poem '72 in the David Hume Tower at Edinburgh University. An undergraduate in Eng-Lit and a real poetry impresario, called John Schofield, persuaded hundreds of people to attend an all-day event, where poets like Norman MacCaig, Robert Garioch, and Adrian Mitchell headlined readings while newcomers like Brian McCabe, Ron Butlin, Andrew Greig and I were put on to do short readings before these luminaries. We were the support acts and had a captive audience. I remember doing ten minutes before Norman MacCaig who, recognising how shy and nervous I was, came and took my hand and led me on stage, so much of a gentleman was he. It was heartening indeed for all of us neophytes to read with – and later drink with – our heroes. What a day! Publication followed for all of us.

Fast-forward to the present. I'm always being asked how poetry is faring in this digital age. It seems to me that it is flourishing. *Be the First to Like This* – I was probably the last to recognise the Facebook reference in the witty and resonant title, I must admit – proves this on every page. Donny O'Rourke's era-defining anthology *Dream State* was published in 1994, and captured and celebrated the spirit of the generation after mine. Never since has there been a single volume that does the same thing so brilliantly for the next group of new kids on the block. Until now.

Much of what I read here was new, but many of the poets herein are familiar to me as people I've been lucky enough to share the stage with. People like the brilliant Rachel McCrum and Jenny Lindsay, who run poetry cabaret Rally and Broad, or Michael Pedersen of Neu! Reekie!, do still invite some of us oldies to read with them. It takes me back to nights with the Lost Poets (as Andy Greig styled Ron Butlin, Brian McCabe and myself) in the Traverse bar at the odd Festival Fringe in the mid-to-late-1970s; or to similar nights in the Third Eye Centre with Tom Leonard, Alasdair Gray, Jim Kelman and sometimes the forever-youthful Edwin Morgan.

I'm delighted to find Rachel, Jenny, Michael and so many others in print here together in this book. Very pleased too to find the great Billy Letford included alongside Samuel Tongue and Nuala Watt, whom I was lucky enough to 'mentor' as part of the Clydebuilt project (and pleased too that royalties from the sale of this book are to go to Clydebuilt). But mainly I'm thrilled to find here in black and white, speaking out loud and clear to me, so much which is brand new and inspiring. Here are plenty of names to watch out for. Performance and voice are intrinsic and essential to each and every poet gathered here. They all know that even poems on the page must speak out, must sing out, into the ear of the reader. Be the first to *listen* to this...

Learning to Love the Present
by Colin Waters

In the autumn of 2012, I was in the audience at a debate held in the Scottish Poetry Library. The debate was called 'What I Love – What I Hate about Poetry', its title inspired by Edwin Morgan's 'A View of Things' ('what I hate about diamonds is their mink / what I love about poetry is its ion engine'). It was an air-clearing exercise: the hope was that by admitting there were aspects of poetry that are hard to like, we could move on to talk about what we enjoy. The debate was an attempt to reach out to people turned off by poetry's reputation for obscurantism or by that odd voice some poets read aloud in. The thinking was, give sceptics a platform to air their complaints and perhaps they'd stick around to hear why poetry isn't a complete waste of time.

The panel included the National Poet of Scotland Liz Lochhead, playwright David Greig, poet Stav Poleg (whose work is included in this anthology), and *Scottish Review of Books* editor Alan Taylor. When asked what he disliked about poetry, Taylor unrolled a list of complaints, one of which stayed with me. He had had enough, he said, of poets writing about landscape, love, nature – the staples or, more damningly, the crutches – as if somehow unaware that generation upon generation of poets had written about the same subjects. He said he was tired of reading contemporary poems 'to a mouse' (the rodent) and wanted to read more poems 'to a mouse' (the piece of computer kit). Perhaps the audience for poetry would be larger if poets gave some sign of living and writing in the same century as readers.

Throw a stone in Edinburgh or Glasgow today and you'll hit someone who runs or has taken part in one of the cities' many regular spoken-word events. Neu! Reekie!, Rally and Broad, Talking Heids, Caesura, 10Red, Shore Poets, Accelerator, Inky Fingers, Blind Poetics, St Mungo's Mirrorball – just a few of the nights combining poetry and (depending on which one we're talking about) music, film and performance pieces, the informal atmosphere helped along with a drink or two. These nights, which are sparky, fun and impressively attended, are in the main organised by and shine a spotlight on young poets, and enjoyed by equally youthful audiences. Slam and performance poetry aren't predominant. The kinds of poetry on show are as different as the nights themselves. Whereas Blind Poetics offers an open mic to poets who have only recently started to write, Caesura focuses on the experimental and Neu! Reekie! lines up big-name poets alongside fresh talent. It's not at all unusual for the likes of Don Paterson, Douglas Dunn and Jackie Kay to share the bill with promising newcomers; these nights are as much a conversation between generations of Scottish poets as they are an excuse for a knees-up.

Spoken-word events are not new and hardly exclusive to Scotland, but their current popularity challenges received wisdom. We've grown so used to hearing that poetry is at best a minority pursuit (and at worst in an advanced state of rigor mortis) that it's easy to overlook the scene that has developed in the Central Belt.

I don't want to hype what's happening; any claim about the popularity of new Scottish poetry has to be set against the knowledge that, added together, audience numbers at the various poetry nights mentioned wouldn't come close to rivalling the turnout for the average Coldplay enormo-dome gig. I'd argue, though, that at these nights you can hear echoes of moments from Scotland's past, times when poetry had a presence on the national stage. The last period to witness so many well-attended spoken-word nights in Scotland was the run-up to another vote to decide the future of Scotland: the devolution referendum in the late

1970s. Reading John Herdman's memoir of the era, *Another Country* (Thirsty Books, 2013), you can see a direct line of ancestry running from today's spoken word events back to a series of events run by the Heretics group of writers and musicians, nights mixing

> the reading of poetry and prose with folk music in a relaxed pub atmosphere . . . [We would] present new and emergent writers on the same bills with weighty and established figures so as to give an overview of 'the poetry and music of Scotland's living tradition'.

Those nights brought together well-known poets – Norman MacCaig, Robert Garioch – with up-and-comers such as Tom Leonard and Liz Lochhead, who, today, fulfil the role of 'established figures' at Neu! Reekie!, Rally and Broad, and the other 'poetry cabarets'.

Now, as then, these nights take place at a time of much discussion about the country's future. Poetry and poets play a part in the independence debate. Liz Lochhead read at the launch of the Yes Scotland campaign. A number of the poets featured in these pages are campaigning for independence. Jenny Lindsay, for example, is an organiser for National Collective, 'the non-party movement for artists and creatives who support Scottish independence'. When Scots are confronted with a major political choice, one that coincides with questions of identity, they talk and argue about it. And poetry is one of the ways in which our nation conducts that debate.

This isn't to say that many of the new generation of poets write directly about independence or 'Scottish identity' – few do (and, apart from Harry Giles's 'Brave', you won't find any in this anthology). What's going on at these nights is not a debate about whether to tick Yes or No in the polling booth. If the poems feed into the independence debate, it isn't through stirring calls to arms. These poets describe the present, the better to take stock of who Scots are. Every poem is a vote of confidence in Scotland as a place of interest and worth. A country might survive having no heavy industry or even national press (as Scotland may soon discover, given the weak sales of its newspapers), but a country without poets is no country at all.

When I was asked to become poetry editor for Vagabond Voices, I said yes because I wanted to publish this book. I was surprised no one else had thought of doing a collection on this scale for this generation of young poets (Donny O'Rourke's *Dream State*, which covered a previous generation, was an obvious inspiration). Through attendance at the poetry events already mentioned, my work as Communications Manager at the Scottish Poetry Library, and reading publications supportive of Scottish writing (such as *New Line Perspectives*, *New Writing Scotland* and *Gutter*), I knew there were many poets just starting out who were worth reading. I wanted to capture them in a book that would act something like a class photo, a yearbook or time capsule.

My first idea for *Be the First to Like This* was to publish forty poets under forty. It has a nice ring. It's the sort of high-concept collection that appeals to literary editors in search of something to fill the gaps between the ads, and guilty booksellers who want to do something to help poetry short of actually supporting it on a day-in-day-out basis.

I scrapped the idea during the early stages of talent-scouting for *BTFTLT* (as I'm going to call it from now on). While the book is largely made up of work by young poets, I chose not to put an age limit on the collection. It would be gimmicky. Besides, I read work by post-40 poets, such as Vicki Husband and Patricia Ace, whose wit and invention could only make the anthology better. Conversely, I read work by twentysomethings so in hock to hoary old tropes it might as well have been written with a quill on a scroll.

'Make it new.' Ezra Pound's (century-old) maxim was often in mind as I read in search of work I wanted to include. I didn't start out with criteria beyond 'find good poems', but my ideas evolved as I ploughed through pamphlets and magazines. I wanted poetry that reflected some aspect of today. I was drawn to verse that was about something I'd never seen addressed in a poem before. I grew suspicious of poetry with one eye on eternity, by which I mean poems that left out references to the present in pursuit of a spurious classicism. I wasn't worried that this might date the poetry. Read enough Byron and Burns and you come across references to people and events that need footnotes. It hasn't harmed their reputation.

I was especially wary of certain recurring subjects. Might I suggest a moratorium on poems about Odysseus? Could poets stop writing about paintings, for a while anyway? And as for hills, clouds, rivers, fields, flowers – there are poems in this collection that feature such things, but always viewed idiosyncratically. Take Niall Campbell's 'The Tear in the Sack', which transforms a simple rural tableau into a cosmic vision within a few lines. Samantha Walton's 'Move away, never come back' spoofs the notion of finding inspiration in a rural retreat. And Marion McCready's 'Daffodil Horns' is a nature poem that unsettles, rather than comforts:

>   we do not understand
> and the daffodils   they spread like cancer.

These are not writers awed by the weight of tradition into repeating Wordsworthian homilies. They trust their own eye and their own era to feed their visions.

So why not write poems about watching TV (like Ross Sutherland's '555'), texting (Michael Pedersen's 'X Marks the Spot'), internet dating (Tracey S. Rosenberg's 'Meeting a Guy off the Internet'), STDs (Krystelle Bamford's 'On

Visiting the Sexual Health Clinic Before Work'), government spending (nick-e melville's 'CU TS'), an MRI scan (Sarah Stewart's 'MRI'), pornography (Janette Ayachi's 'The Annabel Chong Documentary' and McGuire's 'Delta Fos b.') or genetics (Pippa Goldschmidt's 'The Ballad of the Immortal Gene')? People who don't like poetry can't criticise these verses for being remote from reality or for having been written only to be enjoyed by other poets. This ivory tower has broadband.

That's why I settled on *Be the First to Like This* as the anthology's title. I took it from a poem by Theresa Muñoz, who took it from the internet. While the phrase references Mark Zuckerberg's Big Idea, it also describes the way in which many of the poets gathered here will be unfamiliar to readers – although not for long. William Letford will be known to many, his debut collection *Bevel* (Carcanet, 2012) having collected a number of good reviews ('The pleasure I have gained from William Letford's poems alone will, I am confident, stay with me for ever,' Nicholas Lezard, *The Guardian*). Michael Pedersen, the co-creator of the popular Neu! Reekie! night also has high-profile fans ('Michael's poems are so physical you can almost touch the images in them. I adore poetry like this,' Stephen Fry). Those who take part in the Central Belt's spoken word circuit as a performer or audience member will know the poets featured in *BTFTLT*; for everyone else, I hope the anthology will persuade you the scene is promising.

Given the collection's focus on new voices, I gave myself a rule of thumb: I wouldn't include anyone who had published more than two full-length collections. It meant leaving out a number of poets I would otherwise have included. Jen Hadfield, for example – having won the T.S. Eliot Prize, she needs no introduction. J.O. Morgan is another fine poet, but his latest book, *At Maldon* (CB Editions, 2013) is his third.

Now that I've raised the subject of the conditions I

imposed on the anthology, I should explain the subtitle 'New Scottish Poetry'. When it comes to defining who is 'Scottish', I go beyond Alasdair Gray's definition (found in his 1992 book *Why Scots Should Rule Scotland*) – 'By Scots I mean everyone in Scotland who is able to vote' – to include those born, bred and continuing to live and work here; Scots who left the country as children, or later, for work or love or education; and those born outside Scotland but who have made their home here. This anthology brings you the work of Niall Campbell (brought up on South Uist), Ross Sutherland (born in Edinburgh to Scots parents before moving down south as a child) and Aiko Harman (a Los Angelean who made the capital her home after studying creative writing at the University of Edinburgh). Half of the poets I have chosen were born outside of Scotland.

I would like to think that the broadness of the definition is a reflection of national confidence. The debate about who was Scottish thirty years ago was a prickly, contested affair. There were even those who wished to exclude from the official record a native genius like Muriel Spark – she judged herself 'Scottish by formation' – because she had spent most of her adult life outside Scotland. In our more diverse society, it would be more odd to leave out a poet like J.L. Williams (born in New Jersey, a resident of Scotland since 2001 and a UK citizen since 2008) than to include her. Scottish poetry would be greatly diminished without the presence of poets originally from England, Ireland, North America, Mexico, Israel, and so on, who have brought their talents here and done so much to open up our country to alternative ways of seeing and hearing.

The failure of the 1979 Devolution referendum was followed by a decade of Thatcherism, crushing the spirit abroad in Scotland that John Herdman chronicled. I grew up in the 1980s, and recall a time of national low esteem and impotent anger. No one captured the mind-set better than Irvine Welsh did in his novel *Trainspotting*:

> Ah don't hate the English. They're just wankers. We are colonised by wankers. We can't even pick a decent, vibrant, healthy culture to be colonised by. No. We're ruled by effete arseholes. What does that make us? The lowest of the fuckin low, the scum of the earth. The most wretched, servile, miserable, pathetic trash that was ever shat intae creation.

I felt that as a teenager. Many of my peers did. Even into my early twenties, I was surprised when I met someone born outside the country who had made Scotland their home. I don't feel that now. And I suspect most Scots don't feel it either (although you hear a hint of the old cultural cringe in the incredulous immigration clerk who asks, 'Why do you want to live here?' in Theresa Muñoz's poem 'Life in the UK'). Perhaps Scots now believe, as I do, that if we're not the best we're not the worst either, and that there are things that are OK about being Scottish. It's not patriotism so much as it is growing tired of always thinking the worst of yourself, especially in the face of signs that it doesn't have to be that way. There are a number of well-rehearsed reasons for a rise in Scots' confidence since the 1990s, not the least of which was the founding of a national parliament that, while not perfect, has at least refused to go along with the worst excesses of the Westminster Tory-led coalition, such as the bedroom tax. Anyway, I no longer wonder why someone from abroad would want to live here.

There are cultural reasons for confidence too, one of which – ironically – was the phenomenon of *Trainspotting*. The reception that book received gave someone of my generation a first taste of what literature can do for national esteem. Contemporary Scottish poetry is unlikely to repeat the global success of *Trainspotting* – not least because you can't make a film out of it – but it's having its effect locally. When it comes to poetry, we can look any other country in the eye. Between them, Scottish poets (John Burnside, Kathleen Jamie, Don Paterson, Jen Hadfield, Robin Robertson) have won every major UK poetry prize.

We shouldn't get carried away. That passage from *Trainspotting* might feel like it's about a moment that has passed, but there was also a time when those hopeful Heretics nights John Herdman writes about looked as though they'd never return either. Will a slump similar to the one that took place after the failure of the devolution referendum descend if – when? – independence is rejected? Sometimes I think (I'm writing this just over a month before the independence referendum) when I hear the more optimistic claims of the Yes campaign, that they're setting people up to be disappointed, whichever way the nation votes. It's not as if the country isn't already prone to wild mood swings. The tendency even has a name: the 'Caledonian antisyzygy'. This is, after all, the land that produced the author of that split-personality masterpiece, *Doctor Jekyll and Mister Hyde*. I'm reminded of the last line of Niall Campbell's poem 'The Work', included in this anthology, about poets being 'the bringer of the feast and the bill'. Perhaps only a Scottish poet could describe his trade as such.

Even so, I don't believe that another collapse in confidence will ensue if (as the latest polls suggest) Scotland votes against independence this September. Why do I say that? Because of the poetry in this collection. As I've said, the country I live in is different from the one that existed in 1979. Scotland has a parliament, and is in a number of ways already politically and culturally independent of the rest of the UK. The population is also more diverse, and that heterogeneity of background has only strengthened, not diluted, the country's conception of itself. The anthology would have failed if it didn't reflect that.

The poems I have chosen are largely in English, with some in Scots. Why are there no poets who write in Gaelic, Lallans, Shetlandic and Scotland's other languages in *BTFTLT*? It is with enormous regret and not a little shame that I must admit that I can't read them. Blame my education or, if you must, blame me. I am much heartened to learn that on the subject of teaching Gaelic now, pupils are better served that when I was at school. That change, however, has come too late for me. Having never learned Gaelic, I don't trust myself to be able to judge the best new poetry written in it. For a poem to appear in *BTFTLT*, I had to love it and to understand why I loved it.

A word on where money raised by *BTFTLT* is going. Vagabond Voices is paying the royalties to Glasgow's Clydebuilt Mentoring Programme. Clydebuilt takes poets with a track record and pairs them with writers who are just starting out. Over the course of a year, a poet meets with a small group every month and guides them towards discovering their individual voices. The first intake of apprentice poets was in 2008, with Liz Lochhead, Gerry Loose and Miriam Gamble amongst a number of poets who have acted as mentors since then. Graduates include Samuel Tongue, Nuala Watt and Vicki Husband, whose work you'll find in this anthology. By buying a copy, you help to keep the scheme running.

Edinburgh, August 2014

Be the First to Like This: New Scottish Poetry

Patricia Ace

© Bob McDevitt

Patricia Ace was born in Cleethorpes, of Welsh-West Indian parentage, and brought up in England, the Middle East and Canada. She studied English and Drama at the Universities of London and Glasgow before settling in rural Perthshire in 1993 to raise a family. In 1995 she co-founded the female poetry collective Lippy Bissoms. Her work has appeared in numerous journals and won the *Aesthetica Magazine* competition and the Plough Prize. She holds a Masters in Creative Writing from Glasgow University. Her first full collection is *Fabulous Beast* (Freight, 2013). She lives in Crieff where she teaches yoga in schools and the community.

Skye lines

I

a stone – a rock
a single track

an aird – a stack
a dolphin's back

Hallaig – a cairn
a cataract

Sorley MacLean
into the main

II

a cliff – a drop
a long way down

a dun – a broch
a long road home

a fence – a gull
a scallop shell

a coral beach
a pilgrimage

a Cuillin view
a ringing rock

a scarp – a loch
a sunset too

III

harbour – heron
the *Bella Jane*

small lights in boats
jetty – a float

a castle – a keep
sheer drop – steep

a lover's leap
a fishing fleet

IV

a four-winged isle
a daffodil

Trotternish
a splash – a fish

burning heather
passing places

the weather, *the weather*
silence, spaces

a bridge – a sound
a tide – a tor

a wave – a shore
a harbinger

The Clangers on Acid

We were young, in our twenties, living in the country,
on the dole and trying to be artists. Unfortunately
we'd chosen Perthshire, a cultural dearth, the only people
harbouring any creative urge were retired from long careers
at the Council, Hydro Electric, Norwich Union.
So we continued to feed our hollow souls with the usual
suspects – drink and drugs – the baby in bed, *Brookside*
on the tele, a spliff on the go and Ian dropping in from over
the road to show us how to make a chillum out of a carrot.
The three of us huddled round the coal fire like the Fates.

But soon enough we got bored of that and invited friends
from the city for dinner, dropping a tab before
we sat down for starters – the beef in red wine went largely
untouched – really I shouldn't have bothered. Within half an hour
the wallpaper was crawling, the rag-rug a Lilliputian orgy,
embryos bobbed in the lava lamp. An hour in and the girl I hardly
knew but always liked, had thought, in fact, might enact my
lesbian fantasies later that night, was telling me about the
miscarriage she was having in my kitchen. I took a long hot bath
and tried to get a grip. It didn't work.

Within minutes it seemed the sun had come up and the baby
wanted breakfast. We watched *The Clangers* on video.
I was strung out for six weeks after that trip, suffering
delusions of grandeur, convinced I was the next Sylvia Plath,
ready to stick my head in that oven. And the rest?
Mostly we grew up and settled down, got mortgages and proper
jobs at the Council, the Hydro, Norwich Union. The dealer
got MS and died young and that girl, she moved to London,
never carried a child to full term.

Diary in Old Age

New Year's a conspicuous absence,
a week of blank days stretch across two pages
before business kicks in on the 6th:
that week a new car you'll never really learn
how to drive, then a new PC *arrived at 5.00 pm*,
a tax return mailed, a Burns Night, a blood test.

February begins with a bad cold
and an ultrasound, ends with a 24-hour ECG.
In March AOL goes down for five days
caused by *faults on the line* at BT. A mouse
is trapped at the Bowling Club on the 17th,
Broadband installed, *myopathy confirmed.*

Cambridge win the Boat Race in April,
a horse called *Don't Push It* claims the National.
Phil Mickelson, 'devoted father, loving husband',
takes the Masters. Your wife's birthday is logged
with characteristic brevity, CJA – 69.
May brings a Blue Badge but little else of note.

The summer weeks appear a blank wilderness
as Mixed Pairs and Ties are deleted, cancelled.
By June, appointments with specialists
feature strongly; biopsies and bone marrow
extracted by Dr Hunter, Dr Soutar, Dr Gillmore.
Drugs are administered. Writing becomes spidery.

The pages are given over to recording treatments
and symptoms, spates of hiccoughs, poor sleep,
dizzy spells, faints. *Tired all day, shaky / unsteady*
noted in a poor hand. A spell of weakness
in August leads to several entries of *Bed all day.*
Orders for monitors, urinals, supports jotted down.

The last entry, September 2nd, the day of admission;
the time, the Consultant's last name: 12.45 Dunn.

Juana Adcock

© Saule Zuk

Juana Adcock is a writer and translator working in English and Spanish. She was born in Mexico and has been living in Glasgow for seven years. She completed a masters in Creative Writing in 2009. Her work has been included in anthologies and literary magazines in Mexico, the UK, Germany, Sweden and USA. Her first poetry collection, *Manca*, was published in 2014 in Mexico.

X

Conveniently located at the heart of the world
we are a multi-modal transport hub.

Our terminal complex building holds you
in its arms, with soft furniture and newspapers.

Please do not bring cigarette lighters nor other
dangerous items and be patient as we carry out

important security procedures. We work
around the clock providing excellence

in your experience. Our statistics
indicate a steady one percent increase

in our millions of cargo and passengers
handled. The environmental challenge is understood

and minimised whenever possible.
You can dine on the deck as you watch

the aircraft leap off the ground.
We are well connected to the world.

Pennies, or how I single-handedly got us out of the crisis

When I arrived to the so-called united
kingdom reigned by automatons and charlatans my money
soon ran out. I found in the pantry
of the humble hostel that housed me a big jarfull
of brown penny conserve, organic and handmade in a farm in the north
    of France.
From that vital jelly I started stealing, a bit at a time,
to buy a pint of milk, any bread.
I rummaged too
through bins for dispersed spaghetti strands,
for peppers almost rotting.
Often in my last moments of hope
I found in a puddle a heavy pound coin
then I invested it all at once
an offering from the god of money to the god of cacao.
I stole the apples fallen to the pavement
I stole plastic rings from pound shops
I rose at dawn to slave at the till,
the coins that fell as I cashed up
stapling through my temples with their high-pitched
smell of gunshots in lands of other men stolen by other men.
It's not mine, it's not mine, it's not mine, it's not mine, it's not yours,
    it's not theirs, it's not ours.
How many times did I walk for hours for lacking
the last missing penny for my bus fare?
But one day I cracked it: I remembered the jar of conserve, always full,
    no matter how much I stole.
What we needed was to plant pennies on the pavement
to gift ourselves a feeling of abundance—a penny a day
keeps your bad luck away. The sole
speculation magical intention
that transforms self-referencing money
into self-referencing money. The god of Money is circular:
may it not stagnate, may it—meagre as milk—never run out
just like cows when they pour themselves out
or that clear
whisky first currency of Scotland
usige beatha first water of life
pissed out of a cow

Pie Chart on the Global Distribution Of Military Expenditure

The germ of every next
grandma counting
pennies out of her tattered purse
begins with this pie chart.

Operations, sums
where bigger ones
take smaller ones
in.

Watch how colour
affects the perception of size and how
the slices at the forefront appear larger
than what is at the back.

The most elegant charts
don't require data
labeling.

When used properly, they
can persuade anyone.

The parent of armies,
the totalizing *"all the world's languages
will be forgotten."*

With easier access to credit
poverty fuels the tendency
of poverty
to rise.

War is the life-giver, the employment-

maker, the putter-of-food-on-the-plater, the financial market-upper.
She doesn't see it, it's not her fault but the pennies are tiny
life-takers.

Suddenly weakened,
they weaken.

To the first decimal point, the numbers
will seem precise.

Claire Askew

© Helen Askew

Born in Northallerton, North Yorkshire, in 1986, Claire Askew grew up in the Scottish Borders. Her poetry has appeared in numerous publications, including *The Guardian*, *Poetry Scotland*, *PANK* and *Popshot*. Her work has been twice selected to appear in the Scottish Poetry Library's *Best Scottish Poems of the Year* anthology (2008 and 2009), and has won several awards, including the inaugural International Salt Prize for Poetry in 2013 and a special runner-up prize from the 2014 Edwin Morgan Poetry Award. Her debut pamphlet, *The Mermaid and the Sailors* (Red Squirrel Press, 2011) was shortlisted for an Eric Gregory Award in both 2010 and 2012. Claire holds a PhD in Creative Writing and Contemporary Women's Poetry from the University of Edinburgh, and works as a Project Co-ordinator for Scottish Book Trust.

Bad moon

The moon must be sick of being in poems –
always gripped by fingers of late honeysuckle,
always filtered in the lake through the jetty's slats,
always silvering the flicked tails of the koi.
Always a dinner plate or mirror,
always a fingernail clipping, a grin.

The moon must be sick of being in poems.
Always the bright pin in the picture's corner,
always looking in at the windows of middle class homes.
Always shoved above a bridge in Paris or Venice,
always an eyeball or symbol,
always a radiant woman, a bowl.

It's also in the splintered windscreen of the crime scene
with its blots of blood. It's hung over the pig farm,
streaking white across the silo's cheek
and slanting through the lorry walls in blades.
It's in every dented can at the landfill pit,
turning the tip to a shoal of dirty fish.

Never the buried skull,
never the gummed plug in the junkie's sink.
Never the white cat under the truck's wheel,
never the beached and stinking jellyfish.
Never the gallstone or the pulled tooth, of course.
Nobody wants to read poems about this.

Privilege

It's knowing how much cash you can put on a horse
without caring if you win. It's winning,
then giving a little to the man in the doorway
round the side of the track, then telling everyone
at dinner you gave it to him. It's the noise they make
when you finish the tale. It's the cufflinks and the silverware,
a waitress who smiles and takes your coat;
it's whether or not you acknowledge her, that choice.
It's dinner, not really worked for or worried about; the tip
you chuck in the tray on your way out.

It's sitting in the window of a coffee shop, the sun
painting bars across the wooden floor, the plain steel
flip-top teapots shining, writing down ideas that are all yours.
It's walking out of there, blue notebook under your arm,
into the lean summer afternoon without fear,
and choosing which of those ideas you share with whom.
It's in the way the off-license cashier addresses you,
his hazel eyes meeting your own, the fact he doesn't
follow as you head through to the better whisky
lined up in its amber jars.

It's skin you wear each day with all its flaws, adornments;
taut and fine and pale as corset lace, desirable.
Your place on the massive swatch-chart you call race.
It's limbs, their length and shape, the ground you cover easily,
the measured stretch to catch the hard-stitched ball that's thrown,
your fingers maple-leafing out to fling it back. It's the park
where all of this is done, the quiet, clipped grass
apple-pocked; the landscaped trees the afternoon hangs in
like chimes. It's the streets you climb when you go home,
the shutters rolling down as lights blink on above your head in globes.

It's home: four walls you pull around yourself no matter
what the day has done. They're walls you picked yourself
and painted, hung with lamps and scraps and gems,
your things. It's things like this, and simpler: shoes,
a bank account that bears your name, an obelisk
of shelves with books, a fist of keys you didn't steal,
a passport and a roll of coins. It's death,
the one that you will someday get: a grave
to visit, watered, free of weeds. It's all of these:
these hair's-breadth tricks of fortune, birth and place.

Think of it like lucky lotto balls you play each week.
So senseless. Random. Begging to be checked.

Driving in snow

We saw it swallow the hill first.
The sky split and clicked
like a cooling flashbulb:
fizzed with the first flakes,
snorted up whole lines of trees.

It was quick. Even as the starter-motor fired,
the valley was filling itself
like a bathtub, greedy. We skidded
at the hill-gate and slid
a good ten feet – my sister in the back seat
chanting *Shit. Shit. Shit.*

I eased us out without wheelspin
or incident – took off my boots
and socks to coax the pedals,
greasy and cold. I had fifty six horsepower
and a bald tyre I knew
I should have had seen to.

The road was like wadding.
We were the only warm bodies for miles.

Janette Ayachi

© Chris Scott

Born in London to an Algerian father and a Scottish mother, Janette Ayachi is an Edinburgh-based poet who graduated from Stirling University with a combined BA Honours in English Literature and Film Studies. She then received an MSc in Creative Writing from Edinburgh University, and has been published in over 50 literary international journals and anthologies. She has been shortlisted for *Write Queer London, The Young Enigma Awards,* two *StAnza* competitions and a *Lancelot Andrewes Award.* Last year her filmpoem collaboration *On Meeting a Fox* was the official selection for the Visible Verse Festival in Toronto, now featured online in *The Baltimore Review.* She edits the online arts / literature magazine the *Undertow Review,* and reads her poetry around Scotland. She lives with her two young daughters, and is the author of the poetry collections *Pauses at Zebra Crossings* (Original Plus, 2012) and *A Choir of Ghosts* (Calder Wood Press, 2013).

The Annabel Chong Documentary

I am broken into pieces like bread
    passed out, shared amongst the men;
        they take me between their teeth
tasting my consistency in relief
    kneading my body back to dough
        positioning shapes that they know
to savour the places with surprise
    where I rise   where I rise
        or slowly they break in where I bake
scavenging crumbs as my body numbs awake.
    Fucking two hundred and fifty
        men on tape for ten hours
this is my celebration
    of a new woman's liberation.
        Messalina you were my muse
you too had appetite to feed and prove
    even Scylla could not succumb
        to how many men you won,
staining your name in history.
    And now this my documentary
        which to declare equality I endure
as Woman, Asian, Feminist, Whore,
    – the truth of me has been said
        I am broken into pieces like bread
passed out, shared amongst the men.

Hiatus

I found returning your library books
the love letters you never sent

confessing desire for the girl
who cried the most at your funeral.

If you could hear me I would ask
what it is like in heaven,

I know you are watching the world
as you would watch a soap opera,

flicking through the channels of countries
to whatever suits your mood.

So I wonder how you are now
being spirit instead of body

now that weightlessness
has surpassed your waking state.

I battled for your survival
and tried to keep you breathing.

I held your hand until it filled with helium
and almost took me with you.

Airports

Dislodged in a wasteland of waiting
contemplating everything
as messengers preach time and connections
over tannoys, surveillance is implanted in the walls
so that in a control room somewhere
everyone is a digital shadow;
a migrant, a traveller, a terrorist
all waiting our turn to get on board
take off to another city escaping one life
to step into another story.
We feed a limbo of cargo into gluttonous x-rays
our belongings stripped down to bare shapes
as we stand in circles take cylindrical steps
backwards lines fragment, return to the beginning.
The plane's engines surrender their gutturals
spluttering a fuel of song into the ether
an interregnum of language is performed
signals are instructed by the body.
An army of hostesses hosting high hair
high fashion and high eyebrows
walk their suitcases like small dogs
where every surface is a runway.
How long in this postmodern space
existing only as a passing place
where time is suspended, hangs from the beaks
of scavenger birds that drop morsels of time to other places.
Escalators escalate being, we zigzag into various levels
of the cerebrum, engaging with glass
rewiring frayed neurons asking ourselves questions.
I'm convinced even breathing is monitored here
our musculoskeletal choreograph marked
lungs ziplocked with a respiratory stock of reasons
to why it is we are falling out of love
to how long we will be unhappy.

Airports are where the choked heart unclogs itself
where ticket stubs from the screening of our lives
gather into piles like the accumulation of cash,
a wealth of experience corrugated down a dotted line
handing out pieces of ourselves
to board onto the lives of others.
Our passes for ports wedged between fingers
like lime balancing its periphery on ice
in the glasses we place on fold down tables
and linear flight serves premises from one cloud
of emotion to another, such an uncanny sense
of alienation and a longing never to be lonely again.

Krystelle Bamford

© Krystelle Bamford

Krystelle Bamford's poems have appeared in *The American Poetry Review* and *The Kenyon Review*. In 2010, she was awarded a Scottish Book Trust New Writers Award and was shortlisted for the 2011 Bridport Prize. Though raised in the USA, she has been living in Edinburgh for the past seven years.

On Visiting the Sexual Health Clinic before Work

Our neat nurse,
her shoes
like over-floured cakes,
separates us—
boy / girl.
We hold slips to say
we have been less
than careful.

What we hold back
is worth saying now:
this carelessness
had been our broken bread
some small hours before.

       *

The waiting room's light is:

        dark honey mixed
         into pasteurized cream.
  or
        white fat
        cut with vinegar.

  or   (can we say it?)
        both: The honey and vinegar,
        the fat and the cream.
        The cream, fat, vinegar,
        and the honey, the honey,
        the honey, the honey.

Two White-Tailed Lies: The Deer

creep as only deer
can. They don't consider
it creeping, though. They're just
deer, walking. We make their dark eyes
into cups for our heartbreak (the last
day you didn't know me anymore
etc.) but their heavy, gamey hearts
hold only tubers, velvet, bone and teeth,
I suspect. The deer creep
and I will see you soon.

On the Death Mask of Dolly the Sheep

The green field fading
into green, then green.
When she was born
she didn't know
she wasn't the first.
She unfolded, bawling
into the slop, sheathed
in new blood, the punch
of muck in her nose,
each leaf, each shoot
a perfect shock of green.

Jeremy Beardmore

© Jeremy Beardmore

Born in Torquay, Beardmore spent part of his childhood in South Africa. His recent poetry pamphlets include *I'll Slap When I'm Dredd* (This Room Press, 2011), *Just Chapsnax Me* (TSoAG Press, 2012), as well as *Sea Adventures, or, Pond Life* (RunAmok, 2012) with James Harvey and *Animal Crater* (Crater, 2013) with Justin Katko. He's also written YA urban fantasy novel, *Invocation* (Critical Documents 2013). He tries to help Samantha Walton to edit the poetry micro-press Sad Press (sadpress.wordpress.com), and Joe Luna to edit *Hix Eros: Poetry Review*. He is sometimes on Twitter (@jolwalton, @franciscrot, @hixeros), and after this he is on poetry strike.

Song

when I was young it was fun,
we watched the train set together.tiff.
 & when it was later it was better,
we watched the rain wet the heather.tiff.

 'lips; lips arc far along the star-line.
 the possibility of small print
is the supple full extent of it'.þx.
 I wake up with a yucky mouth
full of dreams I
 would wish to yell out but
can't remember how to mean:

 & when I was less young it was best,
 we watched the sun set.tiff, in the West
 (except once, which was odd),
 & you a princess in that light.tiff,
 & I, God.*,
 & at night you'd wield whips & wear leather.mov,
 & I kissed your hand.avi & made a list of my demands.rtf:

 & now that we're not, I think I've forgot,
 or tell what I remember in a ramble.arc,
sets of dentures.jpg, I think we've watched,
 but morning eyes hatch weary scramble.jpg,
 & I forget, I forgot, adventures fade,
 it falls to Fate.* to guess which bits she made up,
 & what I made up, but it's too late,
 & whatnot, & too foolish, & too fucked-up, but,

I remember last night,
 we watched the TV set.jpg together,
because it sank to the hills.jpg & shone on the river.jpg
 & covered it all in *Seinfeld*.jpg in silver.jpg,
 & the light.jpg seemed familiar.tiff,
 so I kissed your brow & made a vow.bat,
 as if I'd ever never.*.
I kissed you.* & I vowed to you.
 *.

Vreakvolksonnet

now sweet, strange Prides whom gob name as the eyes,
umong the economic bad news we
also have seen some more negative signs
in recent weeks – the heal'd pings have real hobbies,
some chavs, we've so much more to lose than chains,
shit, in our lunchours, some counterbobbies,
go we COUNTERKETTLING, like gating yangs,

yawing fingernails, a torsion skyspill
net my dura lex sed lex Nollywood jazz,
AMBROSIA STIFFEN'D like an Whole – an Fill'd
Horizon, of COSMOPOLITAN KILT
composition tool – & we paraphrase –
as pointless to us as cunnilingus on
polka-dot pyjama bottoms is – Vreakvolksong

Waiting for them to go and have coffee together
For Kai Frank-Hara *

institutions of love lag behind
what the body comes up with.
my first dag was a spaniel called
Spangles. he went blind. then
I had a dag called Barry. he
went blind. he used to enfold
the black cat I had called Cat and
make huddled dag love with
the air above Cat's back, maybe gla-
nsing blows through his fur,
I don't know about that, and
ejaculate. this is the kind
of love we could have together.

* Not actually for Kai Frank-Hara. For Sophie.

Lorna Callery

© David Aitkenhead

Lorna Callery is an artist, writer and educator who has a keen interest in concrete and site-specific poetry, visual art and performance. Projects include Polka Dot Punks (2011-2012), a pop-up art gallery in and around Glasgow, supporting emerging artists: a visual art experience combined with live theatre and installation work. Born in Scotland, she has performed in various locations and in many forms including as a statue in Buchanan Street, as a blob of black ink in the Saundhaus nightclub, and as a 'regular skint poet' at various events in Glasgow and beyond.

Pigeon with Warburtons

dead still

no nervous skull-shakes
or scuttle-pecks

still

hiding in doorway shadows
as sun slides
like a drunkard
down dull bricks

head still

a single slice of bread
hollowed out by hunger

a noose of brown wholemeal
round its stretched neck

still

waiting for the rain
to disintegrate this frame
                    or
step out
                    be spotted
by twelve
          dirt yellow
                hungry beaks

Prelude to 24 hour alcohol licensing

Land Services sawdust
over vomit
in Gordon Street

a butcher's shop floor

woodchip sludge
nineteen batches
of red drippings

kebab sauce convulses
in a random rain-dance
upon the pavement

A Piece of Rope

how many words
how many letters
how many vowels

describe what you were thinking

a very fine line
leads
to permanent blackness

the colour black does not suit you

Niall Campbell

© Cara Forbes

Niall Campbell is originally from the Western Isles of Scotland. He studied English Literature at Glasgow University, and in 2009 went on to complete a MLitt in Creative Writing at the University of St Andrews. In 2011 he received an Eric Gregory Award and a Robert Louis Stevenson Fellowship. He lives in Edinburgh. His first pamphlet, *After the Creel Fleet*, was published by HappenStance Press in 2012. His first collection, *Moontide* (Bloodaxe, 2014) is a Poetry Book Society Recommendation and has been shortlisted for the Felix Dennis Prize for Best First Collection. He is the winner of the inaugural Edwin Morgan Poetry Award.

The Tear in the Sack

A nocturnal bird, say a nightjar,
cocking its head in the silence
of a few deflowering trees,
witnesses more than we do
the parallels.
                  Its twin perspective;
seeing with one eye the sack-
grain spilled on the roadway dirt,
and with the other, the scattered stars,
their chance positioning in the dark.

North Atlantic Drift

We lay together in a run bath
and thought over the rowing boat
that neither one was rowing,

the evening berthed at the bath side
with its vowel song and habit
of staying with us for a while.

The low hall light behind us,
implied only where her breast,
her hip, undressed from the water.

That night the usual swell and drift
delivered my old spoilt thought
of whether a life like this is long

or long remembered – the shirts
receding in the corner shadows
dropped as weights, or anchorage.

The Work

If I have to, then let me be *the whaler poet*,
launcher of the knife, portioning off
the pink cut, salt trim and fat, tipping
the larger waste off the side of the boat,
and then to have the poem in the drawer;

or, perhaps, let it be *the poet nurse*,
hearts measured by a small watch, balmer,
washer of old skin, stopping by the door
in the night –
                    or *the oil-driller poet*, primed
for the buried flame and heat, lips to the black,

aware how the oilfields in the evening
are lit like our own staggered desks.
Or, *the horse-trader* or *the smith*, or *the waiter poet* –
offering the choice wine, polishing to the light,
the bringer of the feast and the bill.

Angela Cleland

© Angela Cleland

Angela Cleland was born in Inverness in 1977 and grew up in Dingwall by the Cromarty Firth. She studied English Language and Literature at the University of Glasgow and in 2003 completed a Masters in Creative and Life Writing at Goldsmiths College, London. In 2006 she won the Templar Poetry Pamphlet and Collection Competition resulting in the publication of her pamphlet *Waiting to Burn* (Templar Poetry, 2006) and her full collection *And in Here the Menagerie* (Templar Poetry, 2007). *Room of Thieves* (Salt, 2013) is her second collection. Cleland also writes science fiction under the name Cleland Smith; her debut novel, *Sequela*, was named amongst the *Kirkus Reviews*' Best Books of 2013.

Waiting for Connection

I can see it in the air outside, glowing
towers of data, unenterable, unscalable,
a red ghost metropolis risen up
from the frog-squat houses of the suburbs;
stacked to vanishing point, translucent
rooms full of translucent boxes; air
chirruping with information
– I could scoop it hand-over-hand into my mouth,
stick my face in it, holding my eyes
open beneath the surface, roll in it
until my clothes cling to me obscenely.
Its neon walls flyzap possibilities –
to walk down the street, to leave the house –
and anyway all the libraries are shut,
the shops are shut, the houses are shut
and every lit window in their red brick fronts
is a taunting monitor – IKEA, Facebook,
Twitter, IWOOT, Wikipedia,
Amazon, Google, Google, Google . . .
I need connection, I need stuff
and I need it delivered by 9 a.m.
My fingers, oh my fingers are slivered,
my fingers are slivered by catalogue pages,
my mind by the edge of the dead voice
that apologises over and over for the wait.

The Suburbs

Everything is disassembled,
reassembled at the other end, this end,
where it is so quiet you can hear
the screws that are loose,
the screws that are missing.

My hands are bruised from allen-keying bolts;
the hairs in my ears tickle with the creak of metal on wood.

                              A plane flies over

Sleep here is an isolation tank
during the hours forbidden to flight.
I luxuriate in it, open my mouth
for the night to enter
and embalm me wholly.

And how could I never have realised
we owned so many ticking things?

                              A plane flies over

Your voice is unpolluted,
its frequencies splatter the air,
a Hirstian explosion.
I hear sweet notes that have eluded me
for our eleven years together in cities.

Everything echoes. The air is cold, clear, thin;
zwiebelsuppe, chicken noodle, something Chinese.

                              A plane flies over

The silence prickles, clean of the sounds
I'd ceased to hear in the city:
people talking on the pavement outside,
yawning upstairs, flushing next door,
vibrating the building around us.

I hold my breath – here is the sound:
the turn of the record before the music starts.

A plane flies over

Here, every creak,
every snap
is set apart
given space
as if this is a Gallery of Fine Noise:

This piece – the creeping stop-cock-cough – how much?
It will sound tremendous in my loft apartment.

A plane flies over, a city passing
through, cancels out everything,
fills in the spaces between sounds
like sand, provides a background
for all other noises to hide; stage
hands dressed in black against
a black backdrop.

Cross

Needling of jabs, riddle of ducks and feints,
you wait for a clear target.

It comes, as brief as a spark plug's discharge,
a flash of knicker. You unload

from the pivoting toes of the back leg,
extend through knee, hip, ribs, shoulder, elbow –

you are industrial, a piston, oiled
metal pain. Misjudge

and your attack could be countered,
your nose smacked ice pack absent numb,

worse, your blow could absorb like melt water
into the padding of your opponent's gloves.

Miriam Gamble

© Peter Mackay

Miriam Gamble is from Belfast, but now lives in Edinburgh. A pamphlet, *This Man's Town*, was published by tall-lighthouse in 2007; her first book-length collection *The Squirrels Are Dead* (Bloodaxe, 2010) won a Somerset Maugham Award in 2011. She has also won an Eric Gregory Award, the Ireland Chair of Poetry Bursary Award, and the Vincent Buckley Poetry Prize. Her second collection is *Pirate Music* (Bloodaxe, 2014).

Taking Corners
(beginning with a line by Derek Mahon)

What middle-class cunts we are,
coming in our knickers over the action of the Dyson Baby,
which even swallows cat hair
and makes this house respectable, at last.

See how it snuffles out the very least
of the evidence, sticking its nose
(and how, against ourselves, we cannot help but love it)
into cavities and corners like a po-faced aunt.

How the heart outrides its certainties.
Buoyant as a fool on its sphere-based mechanism,
the body follows through,
ploughing a neat, clean furrow down the avenues of glass.

And are we loosening our snow shoes?
Teetering upon the brink of thirty, I lean from darkness
into the light; from mess to measure;
from (pull the curtains, love!) puzzle to clue.

The New Michael

Do not apologise for this, your Freudian slip,
as you guide me through the sections and the aisles
of the bookshop, introducing me as 'the new Michael'
to clusterings of coffee-drinking staff.
I'm not staying, I'm only passing through –
dipping a finger into someone else's life –

so don't worry. It won't be ruling my life
in a hurry. Each day, in the lunch hour, I slip
into the library, running the figures through
my head, calculating when, not if, I'll quit the aisles
of Kafka's castle, the denomination 'staff'.
For a joke, I start signing onto the clock as 'Michael'.

Weeks pass. I order the new Michael Palin
without asking permission from the Life
and Literature officer. War-footings in the staff
emerge because of it – who hates who, and why. I keep lifting my slips
quietly, but the clean iron curtains are ceding to aisles
and I worry about the risk of passing through

to entitlement, a fixed place. Privately, I resolve to be through
with this before it is too late. Michael
becomes my nemesis, haunting the aisles
with tales of what he's doing with his life.
Photographs of him standing on a slip-
way in Australia appear on the staff

bebo site. A half day is called for regular staff
when his book is published. I am through
the big swing doors when the manager says: It slipped
my mind. You've been here as long as Michael,
now; time for a pay-rise. Life
membership of the union is on special offer for dwellers in these isles –

hand shaking, I sign for it. Through the aisles
and corridors of Africa the world follows your staff.
What was it you were reading – Moore's *No Other Life?*
I start, but cannot see it through. In the see-through
mirror of the future, I'm shopping at *St Michael*,
walking the dog for you, while, casually, you slip

into a taxi, starting your next through-trip, taking life
as it finds you, charming the airline staff from the aisles.
You slip each of them a preview copy, autographed 'Miriam'.

On Fancying American Film Stars

From the big screen, and larger than life for a week or two,
which is all a tangent universe can stand,
we take them home and introduce them to our modest living quarters.

Their baby blues stare out at us at all hours of the day and night,
prompting every manner of ridiculous thought, such as:
'The world is small'; or 'What if Elvis *could* have taken to my mother?';

'I will ride across the desert on a purple roan, or some such,
for anything is possible'; and even that old chestnut,
'There is only one for everyone alive.' The cat mewls

at its perpetually empty bowl, the work piles up on the desk,
but we simply say, with a new-found recklessness:
'This is not the most important thing in my life right now';

'you're a predator, catch your own'. We exist
in the bubble of our making, our souls glistening like celluloid,
by turns rock bottom and on fire. What causes it to disappear?

Who can know, but one day we double-take to find ourselves
filing them away in the rack of lost hopes
with the show-jumping videos and 'twelve easy tunes for classical
    guitar',

the cat purring as it settles on the easy chair, as if to say
'What then, what then', the sky sucking back its thunder-claps
and storm winds, saving only one small cloud, which loiters there,

putty grey, shedding rain like tiny lead balloons
on the pristine terraces. And somewhere else a universe explodes.

Andrew F. Giles

© Mark Sedge

Andrew F. Giles was born in Northampton. He has had work published in *Ambit, Magma, Equinox, Poetry Scotland* and *Gutter* as well as various anthologies. He has written for *The Spectator* and *Scottish Review of Books* and edits online literary arts & culture journal *New Linear Perspectives*. His article 'John Burnside's Poetics of Failure: a Havoc of Signs' appeared in US journal *JERRY*, and he recently appeared alongside Don Paterson, David Harsent and others for the Bristol Poetry Institute conference 'Translating Poetry: the Impossible Art'. He is currently researching poetry and poetics at the University of Bristol.

Going Garbo

It is secret & unseen but under your shirt
you are *alive*, working a panel of pert
buttons with your fingers, as cold coils
of white wire lie & rub against your skin.
The machine whispers, curvature ice thin,
a shield against the grim passing gargoyles
& death's-heads, 1000s of white headphone-
wearing passengers who *want to be alone.*

You forge 100, 200 glittering train miles
in a capsule battered by bomb-lit vials
of light &, unseen, you detect the dark machine
has a long moving cord, a gland, a spiny dart
that sews your inner ear to your inner heart,
whose sound within its deep & glaucous mine
is pearly-eyed and huddled close to your bones.
You float, invisible spectre amongst travel zones.

Henry Lord Darnley, syphilitic

The scots king has a history of disease & a leer
for the past & its face that peers from the stave.
Traitor. Who's to blame for the dark-ended years
& the witchcraft of blood from knave to knave?

When did the boils appears? The pus & the rash?
Was it the chisel-face *seigneur* in the castle park
who kissed so well with the thin moustache?
Was it that forbidden knight back then in the dark

with eyes on an auld alliance? He fell asleep all
night with arms looped tight & suddenly woke
breathing hard boozy medieval breath & hauled
himself up to divine rights, one royal line of coke.

Fill in the gaps. There's a trace of your erogenous zone
on the watchtowers; the signs and symbols burn fire
& one hot sexy mood incubates like death in your bones.
Wild Lord Henry went mad, loopy, they say he was a liar.

Soldier II

Brooke, R., *1914 & Other Poems* (Complete Press,
28th impression, 1920). Restrained, a story of memory,
navy-bound with a firmament of stains, the mess
of years, paint, ink, dust and detritus. Unfortunately,

page 25 to 26 is missing. An enigma. A code of
ruptured spines and dark mottled centres, *have
taken out a favourite page for constant use, J.G.*
written in pencil, bound in yellow paper and saved.

A hard treasure to read upside-down, try to eke out
its mysteries. On earth or undersea an icy corpse
with a face like J.G.'s remembers the late-night rout
that took the tattered page. His favourite. He morse

coded it, bewitched it with blue pencil, hieroglyphed
it with newspaper cuttings. He was its second or third
owner, and like me J.G. lightly lifted the shroud of tissue
paper that covers R.B.'s beautiful profile, his last word,

one word, crouched in a trench. A US soldier, Iraq, Turner,
called it his *clavicle-snapped wish*. What a phrase. Yes.
It made me think, a rarity, being more of a slow learner
these days. I blame all things except myself, more or less.

Turner's page 25-6, present: *the droning engines of midnight.*
Should I remove it? *For constant use, A.G.* etc. The wind
took J.G., page 25-6 in his pocket (it was Brooke's *The Great
Lover*, the last two pages), with this sound on his mind

perhaps as he died. As soon as *Here, Bullet* arrived at home
I was on the phone to M, whose father built R.B.'s tomb
on Skyros. I dreamt of snapped skeletons, whiteness, bones,
and the history of violence – unburied because it died too soon.

M gave a talk to the R.B. society on her father, Lieutenant
Colonel Stanley Casson, who wrote: *Let anyone but me be hit.*
I like the way her eyes sparkle when she sifts through remnants
of Casson, like a bird's. Papers thickly inked, room gloamy, unlit

except for page 25-6 in slow looping letters. Slowly, through
suspended dust, it's clear that death is J.G.'s equal friend,
and this is his epitaph. The re-appearance of a lost book, I knew
it was strange, came later. Turner, Casson, my father's laugh

as he came across J.G.'s book. Weird. Owners past scrawl
their dedications on the inside cover: Marie Jaux or Joux, scored
out in someone's heavy blue pencil, wrote *With gratitude for all
the good you have done me* dated *Londres Juin 1921* in words

of the most delicate form, slightly slanted with g's like scythes;
J. Gwinnell is written centrally with a scruffy marching column
of favourite pages in blue pencil on the left, Pages 20, 24, <u>25</u>
doubly underlined. *For constant use.* J.G., History's son,

foresaw some horror (and what about the scrap of diary marked
Saturday 26 [207-158]? New writing this time: *Garden
Party 20 wounded soldiers. 70 altogether*) and cloaked
it in a strange synchronicity of numbers, a coal-blue distance

in his eyes. J.G – my friend- with your page 25-6 in hand,
R.B is singing *set them as a banner, that men may know*
in your brain! Starlight, engine sputters - here lies man,
his fray-edged secret and the million bony faces of ghosts.

Harry Giles

© Inna San

Harry Giles is a writer and performer from Orkney, living in Edinburgh. He founded Inky Fingers Spoken Word and co-directs the live art platform ANATOMY. He has published two pamphlets: *Visa Wedding* (Stewed Rhubarb, 2012) and *Oam: Poems fae Govanhill Baths* (Stewed Rhubarb, 2013). He was the 2009 BBC Scotland slam champion; and his forthcoming collection was shortlisted for the inaugural Edwin Morgan Poetry Award. His participatory theatre has been programmed by such festivals as Forest Fringe, Buzzcut, NTI (Latvia), Bunker (Slovenia), and CrisisArt (Italy). His performance *What We Owe* was picked by the *Guardian's* best-of-the-Fringe 2013 roundup – in the 'But Is It Art?' category.

Brave

Acause incomer will aywis be a clarty wird,
acause this tongue I gabber wi will nivver be the real Mackay, I sing.
Acause fer aw that wur aw Jock Tamson's etcetera, are we tho? Eh?
Acause o muntains, castles, tenements n backlans,
acause o whisky exports, acause o airports,
acause o islans, I sing.
acause o pubs whit arena daein sae weel oot o the smokin ban, I sing.
acause hit's grand tae sit wi a lexicon n a deeskit mynd, I sing.
acause o the pish in the stair, I sing.
acause o ye,

I sing o a Scotland whit wadna ken workin class authenticity gin hit
    cam reelin aff an ile rig douned six pints o Tennent's n glasst hit in
    the cunt,
        whit it wadna
            by the way.

I sing o google Scotland,
        o laptop Scotland,
                o a Scotland sae dowf on bit-torrentit HBO drama series
                n DLC packs fer paistapocalyptic RPGs that hit disna
                ken hits gowk fae hits gadjie,
                tae whas lips n fingers amazebawz cams mair freely as
                bangin.

I sing o a Scotland whit hinks the preservation o an evendoun Scots
    leeteratur is o parteecular vailyie n importance bit cadna write hit wi
    a reproduction claymore shairp on hits craig,
        whit hinks Walter Scott scrievit in an either tide,
        whit hinks Irvine Welsh scrievt in an either tide.

I sing o a Scotland whit wants independence fae Tories
        n patronisin keeks
                n chips on shouders
                    bit sprattles tae assert ony kin o cultural awtonomy whit
                    isna grundit in honeytraps.

I sing o a Scotland whit hinks thare's likely some sort o God, rite?
    whit wad like tae gang for sushi wan nite but cadna haundle
        chopsticks,
    whit sines up fur internet datin profiles n nivver replies tae the
        messages,
    whit dreams o bidin in London.

I sing o a Scotland whit fires tourists weirin See You Jimmy hats the
    puir deathstare,
        n made a pynt o learnin aw the varses tae Auld Lang Syne,
            n awns a hail sined collection o Belle n Sebastian EPs.

I sing o a Scotland bidin in real dreid o wan day findin oot chuist hou
    parochial aw hits cultural references mey be,
        n cin only cope wi the intertextuality o the Scots Renaissance
        wi whappin annotatit editions,
        n weens hits the same wi awbdy else.

I sing o a Scotland that hasna geid tae Skye,
    or Scrabster,
      or Scone,
        bit cin do ye an absolute dymont o a rant on the plu
        rality o Scots identity fae Alexandair mac Alexandair
        tae Wee Eck.

I sing o a Scotland whit cadna hink o a grander wey tae end a nite as wi
    a poke o chips n curry sauce,
    whit chacks the date o Bannockburn on Wikipaedia,
    whit's no sae shuir aboot proportional representation,
    whit draws chairts on the backs o beermats tae lear ye aboot
    rifts n glaciation
        n when hit dis hit feels this oorie dunk,
            this undesairvt wairmth
                o inexplicable luve,

whit is heavt up,
in the blenks afore anxiety is heavt up
by the lithe curve o a firth.
Whit wants ye tae catch the drift.
Whit's stairtin tae loss the pynt.

I sing o a Scotland whit'll chant hits hairt oot dounstairs o the Royal
Oak, whit'll pouk hits timmer clarsach hairtstrangs, whit like glam-
our will sing hits hairt intae existence, whit haps sang aroon hits
bluidy nieve hairt,
whit sings.

Piercings

It took two looks to see him –
snapped head and loose jaw, silent
moviewise. The boy who broke me in,
my head, my skin, up, said "a break-
down would do you good". The change

snuck him past me, but: same flesh,
same stride. I called; we spoke.
The quick, smiling chat of two
folk who knew inside each other's
mouths, but not heads. I looked hard.

The difference wasn't clear, and then
it was. – The lipring that turned
his pout sullen, hot. The jangle
of earrings I'd buried my face in
as he steel-tracked my heavy

shoulders. The scaffold. The sharp,
shocking stud in his busy tongue.
All gone. In the four years since
he hauled me into a lift, with
"You wanna make out?", he'd pulled

out every metal sign, become
employable, less obvious. I'd paid
ten quid in Camden for my first, made
more holes each time I got depressed.
Got inked. He asked, "So what do you do now?"

if you measure the distance between the teeth they'll tell you

so it turns out the fossil of a cricket
    is a lossless audio codec
is a phonograph cylinder expecting the right
    mandrel and needle
hey Indestructible Record Company you know squat
    against the fossil record

    because the silt was so fine
even the undersides of the wings were preserved
    we could see the ridges of teeth
we cannot contain our glee / it is written all over the news
    that cricket, cricket
after one hundred sixty five million years your single chirrup
    loops from my laptop

    the cricket's song is deeper
than the crickets' of today / he boomed the Jurassic
    acoustic landscape
you can reconstruct behaviours / my boreal songs are filed
    in malleus, incus, stapes
are written in the function of my vast lungs

how terrifyingly airless the oceans would be
    without blue-green algae
my song stems from single-celled
    bloom / a song
of respiration / a song / a song / a vibration
    through populous strata
    through one thousand ninety three patents
    through dissected organs
and digital models / now crickets sing beyond our hearing

Pippa Goldschmidt

© Bob McDevitt

Pippa Goldschmidt grew up in London, and now lives in Edinburgh. She is a graduate of the Masters course in creative writing at the University of Glasgow, has a PhD in astronomy and worked as an astronomer for several years at Imperial College, followed by posts in the civil service including working in outer space policy. In 2012 Pippa was awarded a Scottish Book Trust / Creative Scotland New Writers Award. She has been writer in residence at the ESRC Genomics Policy and Research Forum and also at the School of Physics and Astronomy, both based at the University of Edinburgh, and in 2015 she will be writer in residence Hanse-Wissenschaftskolleg in Bremen, Germany. Her first novel, *The Falling Sky* (Freight, 2013) was runner-up in the Dundee International Book Prize. Find out more at www.pippagoldschmidt.co.uk

From the unofficial history of the European Southern Observatory in Chile

When our war is over
we go to Chile
buy a mountain in the desert
build telescopes
with the power to detect
a naked flame on the Moon

Here
the sky curves closer to the Earth
galaxies lightyears away
are observed
young stars shrouded in dust
are revealed
new comets
are discovered
recorded
catalogued

But we can't look at everything
the Moon is too bright
Jupiter burns our camera
we avoid explosions in the South

We run out of things to see
so we invent new things
dark matter to stop galaxies flying apart
dark energy to speed up the universe
but we can't find these dark things

Our telescopes have the power to detect
a naked flame on the Moon
or a light shone by a soldier
into the face of a prisoner
in a camp not far from
here

Here the lone and level sands stretch far away
but I'm no Shelley writing Ozymandias
I'm only *Goldschmidt et al.*
I publish what I see

I can't see the dark things
planes bombing the presidential palace
explosions in the South
camps hidden from view

This is one problem which we cannot solve –
find x
where x is equal
to the number of people
buried in the desert
not far from
here

Physics for the unwary student

1. Imagine that you are trying to balance on the surface of an expanding balloon. List all the different ways in which this resembles reality.

2. Thousands of sub-atomic particles stream through you night and day. Does this account for those peculiar flashes of light you sometimes see?

3. You are trapped in a lift which is plummeting to the ground. Describe what you feel.

4. You are in a spaceship travelling towards a black hole. As you pass the event horizon and become cut off from the rest of the Universe, what do you observe?

5. What happens if you stop believing in gravity? Will you slide off the Earth?

6. What happens if you stop believing?

The ballad of the immortal gene

In the beginning was the flesh
and the flesh was made word

What type of animal turns its body into code
translates analogue mouths
and their inexact kisses
to base alphabet
transforms the electric gradient
between will and desire
to mute letters.

The instructions for our experiment
should be followed to the letter,
these footprints of the dance arrows
on the page,
the directions to turn this way and that
'Keep the head aligned with the neck,
the back, the pelvis, the hips.
The lips.'

Do not forget the lips.
I must place my hand
in the hollow of your back
tuck my head into your shoulder
and sigh with happiness.
I must sigh the base note of desire.

At the beginning I get it wrong
a slip of my tongue on your body
miscalculates the instructions
the beautiful error propagating
possibilities of us into our future.

Now we're too good at following
and not leading
we can't make up new steps
only our bones survive
the soft flesh is long dead now.

Once I understood you
as well as the story of you
we managed to live
in the gaps between our words
between the diagrams on the bedsheets.

'Take your partner's hand'
and so I still hold onto you
you're deposited and sequenced
I have your letters down pat
now that it's too late.

Aiko Harman

© Aiko Harman

Aiko Harman is a Los Angeles native now living in Scotland where she completed an MSc in Creative Writing at the University of Edinburgh. She has lived in Japan, teaching English to high school students and spending time with her maternal family. Harman's poetry has been published in *Anon*, *Edinburgh Review*, and *Fuselit*, amongst others.

In Mobius

The three chasing arrows pinned man to the planet.
Collection, process, use. Each manufactured good
became a tear in the fabric of mankind.
Countries fought to choose who'd bear the cost
of all recycling. The market remained volatile.
The war had milked the land of raw resources.

Efforts flagged. The Ragmen scavenged the last bits

of parchment, metal, terrafibre, cut rubber, ore-fire.
The last classic Chevy Syntex was scrapped in '39.
No heirloom silverware or cherished love letter

tucked up in a cupboard could be spared.
A crime against country, those few
who found 'holding' refused to share
their stash of family photos, kept wrapping paper,
or relics of styrofoam food packaging.

By the '40s, there was nothing. Those who cared
for the planet, bore the brunt of the post-war front:
growing environmental concern and an ever-increasing
post-Boom generation of elderly left most hopeless.
*How would we feed the people if we could not fuel
the Machines?* They conserved energy. Studied
biodegradables. Searched for unthinkable fuels.
Could *Man* be a resource? The strong went dormant,
hid underground, but stalked at dusk, scavenging
the fallen. The kerbside collections began:
the young left their dead at first darkness to be taken
for the good of mankind, *the good of the nation.*

The number of recycling programmes increased.
Approximately 8 thousand routes ran in '51.
Twenty million tonnes composted, fed by truck-full

into the gullet of the Machines.

The Diplomats preached the Old Words from memory:
Recycling reduces the raw materials required.
Maintain core levels to minimise risk to humans.
The ultimate benefits are clear:
clean air, water and better health for all.

Soon the missing persons lists became untenable.
The online cache overflowed with poster atop poster
pleading, 'Have you seen this man?', 'Where is my mother?'
Notices of 'How much for an 86-year-old? Uplift included.'
were quickly taken down but not unnoticed.

The population purge near completion, and 'stock' depleted,
the Machines ground to a halt. The planet bereft
of all resources, no tumbleweed or stray sheet of paper left
to flutter across the empty city streets, silence
became a vacuum.

Few of Those Who Remain remember the old world.
They seldom speak, live alone, forage what they can,
and build nothing.

Immortal Jellyfish, *Turritopsis nutricula*

The scientists are scared: your cycles repeat forever.
The only known metazoan to return completely
to sexual immaturity after reaching the medusa stage.
A feat we can only dream of: slip into our younger skin,
start again, pull a Ponce de Leon, sup from the fountain
of youth ad nauseam.
                          No wonder they fear you,
agile bell, the size of a thumbnail, a postage stamp.
You turn back the hands of time. Skip death.
Your bright red gelatine heart, the cross
at your cusp, invisible dart. So many leagues deep,
the teeming seas, a silent invasion.

How the Beasts Survive for So Long

The surgeon is stealth.
He weaves his fingers between slick gears.
Scalpels the loins of a digit, tweezes an ear.
The surgeon calls to his assistant,
ever-ready at attention, red light engaged,
'Hand me the synatines, post-haste.'

Poor choice of words, as she has only clamps
by which to transport the necessary technology.
Nor is she a *she* at all, but that's beside the point.
The point being, the surgeon is stealth.

His stealth hands delve sprocket-deep
into the lifeless beast, a beast of ill-proportion,
and currently non-functioning magnitude.

The surgeon stealthily syncs the synatines
into the beast's neosyntax. A shock-flare
torques from its open core cavity, nearly singeing
the surgeon's hair. But the surgeon is stealth.

The beast begins to stir, reanimating.
The time is now. Speed is everything.
Like an animal raised in captivity, the key
to returning the beast is stealth.
The surgeon wires the farynx to wazine,
feeds the leaks. The beast's strength is levelling.
The surgeon flashes the corboxin, ties the fan
back into the pin. He wraps the skin taut

onto the titanine and welds the flap shut.
He dives aside in time to avoid a throaty thwap
to the gut. The beast is up.

The surgeon is stealth and has moved by now
into the core regenerator. His fast hands
are already dust, translating through space.
The surgeon has already reformed, behind
the two-way plexitane, in time to watch the beast
ravage the surgery. His poor assistant in bits
amongst the rubble. The beast already boring
a beast-sized hole through the safety hatch
to freedom. But the surgeon is stealth
and the surgeon will save them all.

Colin Herd

© Camila Cavalcante

Colin Herd was born in Stirling in 1985 and now lives in Edinburgh. He is a poet, fiction writer and critic. His first collection of poems was *too ok* (BlazeVOX, 2011). A pamphlet, *like*, followed in 2011 and a second full-length collection, *Glovebox* (Knives Forks and Spoons Press, 2014). He has published over 60 reviews and articles on art and literature in publications including *Aesthetica Magazine*, *3:AM Magazine*, *PN Review* and *The Independent*. He has read and performed his work widely, including at Rich Mix Arts Centre, The Fruitmarket Gallery, Gay's the Word Bookshop, Edinburgh University, and the Edinburgh International Book Festival.

cumbernauld

"nineninetynine" films greenrig road and
uploads it with the caption: "another dumpy
street". a former resident called "multicoloured"
comments "it didn't used to be so jakey".

others film the town centre and complain and
still more film the christmas lights and call the
video "why bother". the word dingy comes up
a lot.

one stylish video with jaunty jerky unpredictable
camerawork uses jimmy soul's "if you wanna be happy"
as a theme tune while touring the sodden carbrain
underpasses and then subtly speeds up the pace of
shoppers's gaits as they trundle past store fronts and
up escalators.

the camera then moves forward and a load of
shoppers are kind of swept into its path and the
video cuts to show children playing.

the carbrain boyz are a gang of 13/ 14/ 15 year olds
who make videos of themselves downing a buckfast
in one swallow and then dancing merrily and sweet.

a very daring cumbernauld high school student is filmed
de-panting his teacher at the blackboard, who then chases
after him enraged, as they move off camera.

the bryce family have uploaded a family video
from 1963 playing in thick white greenfaulds snow, using
it to build a fort or a castle or something. maybe a
town centre.

eva longoria

suffers from allergies. in fact, she's suffered
her whole life from them. "if someone
were wearing perfume next to me, i'd sneeze
and sneeze and sneeze" she said.

strange then that she designed
and branded a perfume herself, called,
elegantly, 'eva'. it's a harmonic blend of
citruses, bergamot, neroli,

aldehydes, jasmine, lily of the valley, freesia,
leather, musk, amber and sandlewood. 'eva'
is available in 50 and 100ml stylish glass
flacons designed by wilhelm liden, paul meyers

& friends, with manufacturer bormioli luigija.
besides this perfume, another fragrance with
eva's name was launched recently. it was
created in cooperation with l.r. health and beauty

systems group and it belongs to the forbidden
fruits collection which includes 4 fragrances
inspired by 4 desperate housewives.

can it be true that emma thompson is allergic
to daisies? or that dougie poynter is allergic to
camels?

the rebrand

it began because you
pretended to forget why
we'd gotten started in
the first place.

we looked up one day.
me from something;
you from something else.

we said: "we're working over
our image. it's simple. it's got to be."

and it kind of was, to
start with.

out with the alcopopblue
in with jadedplum or
better still pistachio.

out with ikea and in with
a single extortionate ebay
hans wegner chair, and the rest,
ikea.

out with fan sweaters from
the band health, in with paul
smith.

out with paella, in with
tagines. and quinoa.

out with ron padgett, in
with ron silliman.

ok we didn't go that far.
but we were getting on ok. it
was all definitely 'us', and
friends remarked on the fact.

but at one point, me on one
self service till, struggling to
get a tin of paint to scan, and
you, balancing a coiled up rug
on the scales,

we looked at each other and
pretended to forget why we'd
gotten started in the first place.

Vicki Husband

© Suzanne Motherwell

Vicki Husband's poems have been widely published in literary magazines including *Gutter, Magma, Northwords Now, Iota, The Rialto* and *The SHOp*, and have won prizes in the Mslexia poetry competition, the Edwin Morgan international poetry prize and the Pighog / Poetry School pamphlet prize. Born in Edinburgh, Husband completed a MLitt at Glasgow University in 2010, and went on to be mentored by Alexander Hutchison on the Clydebuilt poetry apprenticeship scheme. She is a member of the St. Mungo's Mirrorball network of Glasgow poets. She blogs at vickihusband.wordpress.com

Jean's Theory of Everything

She asks them to leave the door open and from her bed calls
the garden in. A brash wind is the first guest bringing a party
of others: soil, leaves that frill the skirting, smells and rubbish
make themselves at home. The roof gives up, lets the rain join in
and through frail panes the sun sits a while, empty handed.

Slugs traipse all night across her floor. She thinks they're fat
and what a waste of time making a marathon trip only to be burst
by the beaks of birds, to slouch to sticky puddles. Seeds scatter
themselves like poor punctuation, taking root in the rug. Soon
green shoots poke through, and worms doing morning yoga.

By winter the lens of her eye has a coating of ice, giving her
a convex gaze. Now she can see the microcosm of things:
parasites living on the hairs of mice, and the architecture
of skin. Nature is a grafter, she grants it that; its work
cut out just keeping tabs on all those leptons and quarks.

She feels much better when gravity lifts, like a hospital blanket
it was too heavy and not very warm. On discovering she is curled
around other dimensions, her vertigo disappears and it explains
that recent trouble with word search. She's also comforted to learn
her tinnitus was actually Cosmic Microwave Background Radiation.

Jean networks with dark matter and finds him to be a nice chap
holding down a job. She has yet to meet dark energy but no wonder,
the expansion of the universe is a thankless task. She can empathise
with this as she moved house many times before her fifth child
was born. Then Jim had the op and the extension was built.

Now she's on the Nomenclature Committee, as the physicists lacked
an adult approach. She feels like the Queen every time a quantum
discovery sails off with the title she gives it. Inspirations include
martial arts and founding members of the W.I. She considers
her other poor selves working dead-end jobs in alternate universes.

At night she could watch the nebulae for hours. She prefers them
to soaps and feigns shock as they sow their stellar seed into space as if
it never happened in her day. Constellations flick past like an album
of old photographs; she reminisces about light when it was young.
It is around this time Jean conceives her Theory of Everything.

What Do the Horses Think?

What do the horses think
on a Saturday night in Glasgow, walking
the trough-like alleys, shadows saddled
with luminous riders? Drawing the city
in draughts through their nostrils, they sift
for the heat of crime, the creature-scent
of humans, the reek of waste. Ears swivel
to catch the lone song of a drunk, wild call
of the pack, first tremor of a stampede.

Passers-by may think
they've imagined these shapes, or conjured
them from the past; horse-shoes ringing
on cobbles echo off steel-trees, vertical lakes
of glass. Do they fantasise of clover fields,
nose-bags, blue skies and sweated miles;
or later, safely stabled, will they re-live
the night: steering a baying crowd
into sticky pens, ghost-drawn carriages?

On Being Observed

When I woke up she asked me what I'd been smiling at
as I slept. Was it dachshunds? she said. No, I replied
I'm pretty sure it was a dream about organisational change
at work. The treads of the steps to our office grew narrower
and we all had to wear smaller shoes. But the smiling?
she asked. Oh, I was probably just being polite.

Russell Jones

© Russell Jones

Born in Gloucester, Russell Jones is an Edinburgh-based researcher, writer and editor. His first collection of poems, *The Last Refuge* was published by Forest Publications in 2009. He is the editor of *Where Rockets Burn Through: Contemporary Science Fiction Poems from the UK* (Penned in the Margins, 2012) and a guest editor for *The Interdisciplinary Science Reviews* (Poetries and Sciences in the 21st Century, 2014). *Spaces of Their Own* is a collection of Jones's science fiction poems (Stewed Rhubarb Press, 2013). Jones has also published on the poetry of Edwin Morgan. A full-length poetry collection, *The Green Dress Whose Girl is Sleeping*, will be published by Freight Books in 2015.

After the Moons

We came upon the plasma fields
accidentally. Our rockets burned
through the atoms of littered space, the dead.
We searched among the debris, hauled

their bodies on board. There were so many
we almost lost ourselves among them,
but in their radiation hardly recognised
the dimming lights they had become.

The scavenge order came, was carried out
smoothly. We burned the bodies, silent, roaring.
Through our windows their planets floated
like ice in a glass of bourbon. No morning

felt so dark in all that matter. We drifted
through the voids that angels could not
fill, rolled, shifted at the glances
of rock that hurtled past. We prayed, shot

photons into the deep emptiness.
What a strange grace. The captain broke
as he often did, his own dead world flooding
back to him. He played a recording

of a fog horn through the ship. Some decision
that was, billions of miles from any sea. In time
we settled by a lake of mercury, scattered
the remains, said our *bon voyage*. As we left

we saw natives cowered in knots, edging
to the mound of ash we'd left behind, bracing
as our thrusters brushed them outward. Our tools
were quiet once again in our safe darkness.

No lights flickered, the consoles lay lifeless.
And there was barely a word between us.
New moons were calling and we knew that
taking debris could be hazardous.

Breathing Space

Stars, don't start.
Leave me to everything.
Burn away. Your glimmers
have made their point
though it's lost.

Let me freewheel
in your distant light,
handstanding, vaulting
through the folds
of your surveillance.

If we'd wanted to see you
every minute of every night
we'd not have built houses,
built factories to drab your sky.
This is our canopy, our cloth
between your vastness
and the immediate universe
of our eyes.

The Flat Opposite

He watches the television at night,
absorbed as she strolls behind him
cradling a dozen tea-candles, alight
in the washroom. She sets them on the rim
of a drawn bath, steam silhouetting her
in the frost of the jarred window. She strips,
the small lights dancing on her skin, a blur
of dreams as she arches, lowers her hips,
breasts, her neck beneath the surface. One hour
passes without consequence until she blows
out the flames and dresses in the flowers
of white smoke. She stops at the door, frozen,
flawless. He flicks through channels as though
he's never seen the goddess through my window.

Dorothy Lawrenson

© Dorothy Lawrenson

Dorothy Lawrenson was born in Dundee, and studied Fine Art at Edinburgh College of Art and the University of Edinburgh. Her paintings are held in private collections, and in the Shetland Contemporary Art Collection. She is editor of the award-winning Perjink Press, and her own poetry is published in the chapbooks *Under the Threshold* and *The Year*. She is currently undertaking an MFA in Poetry at Texas State University.

Leaving Fife

Kingdom of Leven, Ladybank and Leuchars;
you are to me like some eccentric uncle,
with your strange suggestive hills,
your round ravilious fields,
and that black hole left by coal at your heart.
With those pretty edges you look like a doily
for the cities to rest their long spoons.
Paunch above the central belt,
fat with fields of yellow rape,
links and scores,
pig-farms, pantiled cottages,
small stranded villages,
Pit-this and Kil-that.
Your modesty exceeds Dundee's;
your tourist board's logo is the high road south.
What can I say? I'll follow the lead
of a Crusoe, a painter, a millionaire,
and – in this order – love you, and leave you.

Viewmaster

The whole world came in envelopes:
Niagara Falls in Winter,
Wild Animals of Africa,
Paris II. Useless for days,
until the machine arrived.

On the sixth day I discovered
its dated futuristic shape,
its warm brown weight,
its Belgian, Bakelite appeal.

I've always liked kinetic watches,
wind-up radios,
the manual and mechanical.
Each pull on the little lever brought
another scene to all but life:

waxworks in fifties slacks
open-mouthed at Niagara's frozen roar;

gridlock at the Arc de Triomphe;

a leopard motionless,
about to spring.

At length my arms ached like Atlas
holding the world up to a halogen sun,

feeling nearly a god,
the whole world almost in my hands.

The Nerja Caves

Nerja in winter, a hiatus of a place,
the tourist trade's fallow season.

We lay awake through a redundant siesta
as if in solidarity with the lispless locals'

enforced holiday. CNN's interminably breaking
news was muted since we'd got it off by heart.

Buenas said the old man in passing, dropping
the word on the stairs like ash off his cigarette;

the handyman in his newspaper hat,
whitewashing the drained poolside, dragging

out the job for the length of our stay.
We'd said we could afford to miss the caves.

The wind scraped the plastic
sunbeds across the terrace

and later we heard next door's
muffled quarrel on a loop.

In the morning we took the tourist trail.
But certain sights can render clichés new:

I reached for *labyrinthine, gothic, byzantine,*
I could believe in *measureless to man*

inside this giant geode,
these calcite forests,

a mountain range turned inside
out, cathedrals on cathedrals,

curtains, weird flags, sponges
clustered or hung up alone like heavy jellyfish;

the threat of centuries massed overhead,
the breathless, compressed vastness.

That such heights could tower below ground,
such emptiness expressed by what contains it.

Outside the sky seemed
wasted, the sun unfocused.

We checked out on Valentine's Day,
the empty pool now a flawless aquamarine.

The old man put on his desk clerk's hat
to wish us *buen viaje*.

Touching down at Edinburgh is like coming up for air,
or waking from a siesta to find the weather's broken.

And it's as if we've just put back
the time that we took out;

as if we'd never held a breath,
never been afraid to let it go.

William Letford

© Seppi Preston

Born in Stirling, William Letford has an M.Litt in Creative Writing from the University of Glasgow. He was the recipient of a New Writer's Award from the Scottish Book Trust and an Edwin Morgan Travel Bursary which allowed him to spend three months in the mountains of northern Italy in 2008, helping to restore a medieval village. His first collection is *Bevel* (Carcanet Press, 2012). He lives in Stirling.

Be prepared

wear three T-shirts and one hooded top
layers are important
they can always come off
remember your oilskins
it's always raining somewhere
wear a scarf
cold air moves down from the neck
wear gloves
they're useless when wet
but handy if you hit the wrong nail
pay attention to the moment
the way water drips
the way a spider scuttles
have a healthy fear of heights
when working from a ladder
know which way to fall
railings and slabs are unforgiving
flower beds and fuchsia bushes are better
practice your scream
if you strike your thumb with the hammer
don't squeal
roar like a lion
when the pain subsides and you look around
you'll know exactly what I mean
acknowledge the moon
it was part of the earth once
its loneliness can make you feel beautiful
lift properly
you'll need your back to make your money

A bad day

For thousands of years the great civilisations
considered manual and mundane labour
a punishment
Then they abolished slavery
and began the slow process of brainwashing the minions.

Thurs hunnurs a burds oan the roofs

here huw chouf wouf wee robin rid tit peejin breesty lovey dovey
ruffle yur feathers show me yur plume look it that Frank nut a look
nut a nut plod on then mouldy breed heed woop woop look it that
fingle foogle boogaloo that's no even a crow that's a dinosaur
thur'll be teeth in that beak that's fur sure ohh beady eye beady eye
get behind the gable she's fae the social wit a life Frank wit a life
feedin oan scraps huntin fur crumbs bit listen tae this listen tae this
we're no dodos we kin fly forget aboot the fields Frank look it the sky

Jenny Lindsay

© Alex Aitchison

Jenny Lindsay is a poet, performer, and promoter of spoken word, based in Edinburgh. Growing up in Maybole, South Ayrshire, she began her career as a singer-songwriter, before going on to become a finalist in one of the first Big Word Poetry Slams in 2002. She has continued to perform and compere at events across the UK. Her debut collection was *The Things You Leave Behind* (Red Squirrel Press, 2011). Her most recent pamphlet is *The Eejit Pit* (Stewed Rhubarb Press, 2012). She is one-half of literary cabaret duo Rally and Broad, alongside fellow poet Rachel McCrum.

Edinburgh

Edinburgh, Oh Edinburgh…

Edinburgh, you old tart, trussed up in fairy lights,
trancing those curious ones with your curios
and tartan bric-a-brac.
Your knickers out to dry, hanging aside the rest – your
  dirty washing flaps
as your packaged history blows. Wind seeps through
back-alley ghost tours and matching American tracksuits.

Edinburgh, you rebel child,
a glass affronted mock to your elders.
Those eye-sore panics you've erected
shocking the heart of your big brothers.
Edinburgh, you cobbly codger,
You completely unremarked-upon eccentric.

Edinburgh, you Bacchanalian dream,
for pagans and dreadlocked fire eaters.
Alongside a career in buy-to-let,
Nudity forges with superiority . . .
Painted green or blue or red
you turn around to your naked friend
Atop a hill you burn the flame
of new religion – old superstition.

The lines that draw. The needles take.
The streets where shopping trolleys carve
mark the way
from kitchen sink chic
to broken windowed chip shop REAL.
Carve away from class tourists and trustafarians.
Not all roads lead to Princes Street.

Your controversial masonry,
Your sniggeringly greedy cash registers,
Your five pound pints of Peroni,
Your artists and your poetry.

Edinburgh – you Apple pie bed.
You warm and scratchy shocker.
How we walk you –
gingerly, like a first attempt over burning coals,
it's all about the pressure
you put on the surface.

No Ball Games

Donny, 8, trundles outside to play,
Thighs rubbing together from chocolate bar breakfasts.
I think he's pondering in a child's way if anyone will save him.
He shouts 'fuck off' at a seagull.

'Whit?'
He sits on the steps and waits.
Glowers at a scandalised passer-by,
Bouncing his ball against the wall underneath
the blind eye above the hated sign.

That blind eye above that hated sign.
He stares as I pass to leave my work; his life.
I say 'hiya!' as you do to children;
Overly cheery.

He stares. Thinks something impenetrable.

And I'm thinking:

I want to read you bedtime stories!
I want to expand your imagination!
I want to feed you greens and
Expand your horizons and...

AAAAAAAAH-YAH!!

Donny's ball lands a cracker to my temple,
I look back, hurt, unfairly targeted, embarrassed.
Doesn't he know how much I care?
He smiles, underneath the hated sign.
Small pleasures. Small victories.

No Ball Games.

Wisest Is She

You know how it feels when even bones become a burden,
And the last gasp chance lies in God's salvation,
You know about acceptance and the Holy Trinity,
And the best way to interpret Revelations.

You know how many gags it takes to get gawks,
You know where to press and to punch in the abdomen,
You know how many tiles must be counted 'til, psyched up,
The honey is spilt and the milk non-existent.

Magician of worlds you can't contain,
Devil at your back feeding nightmares of beauty,
You know about the hell-fire myths and the sympathy,
That comes from admitting *You know?* . . . *I can't* . . .

And I know *but nothing*, you cry 'til the Heavens,
Still un-opened wag fingers at laments and prayers
For forgiveness, for desecrating that temple,
Your body breaks under the weight of its weightlessness.

MacGillivray

© Christian Thompson

MacGillivray is a writer, musician and performance artist. Under her birth name Kirsten Norrie, she has a Doctorate in Performance and Scottish Identity, for which she studied at the Ruskin School of Drawing and Fine Art, University of Oxford. Her poetry has been published in *New Writing Scotland*, *Test Centre*, *To Gypsyland* and *Magma*. She has performed alongside writers such as Alan Moore, Don Paterson, Brian Catling and Iain Sinclair. Her first collection is *The Last Wolf of Scotland* (Pighog, 2013). As a musician she has worked with Shirley Collins, Arlo Guthrie and The Fall and is releasing a 12" EP in January 2015 and a dulcitone album in summer 2015, both through Hundred Acre Records. Her last album was favourably reviewed in *The Wire* and comprised part of the film soundtrack for the second film she has worked on with British director Andrew Kotting, *By Our Selves*, with Alan Moore and Toby Jones. She is completing a non-fiction work, *Scottish Lost Boys*, supported by Creative Scotland funding.

Lobo

One hundred and twenty years ago Ernest Seton, watercolourist and hunter who claimed his ancestor had killed the last wolf of Scotland, trapped a strong and intelligent wolf he named Lobo after tracking him for weeks. Lobo tripped traps, scatted on strychnine and overturned poisoned meat. Eventually Seton brought Lobo in by killing his mate Blanca. Lobo followed the body of his partner and was caught by Seton who couldn't bring himself to kill the animal. Lobo died that night of his own accord, held in a barn. Seton never fully recovered.

Those water wet paints,
chocked pastel hocks,
he night-brained and dying
in the slatted pen of love.

I laced her with strychnine,
but the bullet melted first,
her young thudding chest.

He in the dust, those wildlife eyes
I dare to touch,
that strong hymnal lurch.

Whitman never saw him there,
wolf locket,
small throat piece, printed with defiance.

I saw him turn his streets off,
take the cusp of dawn to his chest like a drink,
and turn in wait, lying East.

Ghost Dance

And any cinema will seize them,
gripping face lamps hanging open,
outlanders come in late to watch,
feeling for the cheap seats.

On screen, meanwhile, in multitude
men cull buffalo
bar one, loping front of scene,
eyes excretion: oil-on tears,
flailing, plunges, caricature

of nothing
that would lens-wise daze us,
save lone, acclimatising darkness.

outlanders - strangers

Photograph Of Spotted Elk

Who is this man
pulse crunching cross my pillow
I hear him in the snow, right ear-side
in the stupor-stalked night.

Whose half-hearted keffel's desertion
in the dark digresses.

A frozen flag,
in black and white,
held spartan wrist – blank question mark –
of pixillated winter face.

keffel - an old or inferior horse

Richie McCaffery

© Gerry Cambridge

Born in Newcastle, Richie McCaffery lives in Stirling and studies and works as a teaching assistant at the University of Glasgow. He is working on a PhD in Scottish Literature, looking at the Scottish poets of World War Two. He is the author of two poetry pamphlets, *Spinning Plates* (HappenStance Press, 2012) and *Ballast Flint* (Cromarty Arts Trust, 2013). His debut full-length collection is *Cairn* (Nine Arches Press, 2014). His poems have appeared in journals and anthologies such as *The Dark Horse, Stand, The Rialto* and *The Best British Poetry 2012*.

The professional

You ask what I do for a living
and I don't think I can say.
There is something in the way
I take this teacup from you
without the tell-tale click
of ring on hot porcelain.

You ask, *Will this take long?*
Maybe. My questions must
be answered. Some are pointless
as wasps and the pain they give.
Others will take you many lungs
to satisfy the depth required.

Remember my dolphin smile,
my signature like snake-crossed sand.
You will notice some day soon
all your cups carry my trademark –
a faint hairline crack. I specialise
in subtle, half-bearable damage.

Spinning Plates

My mother was mad as mercury,
mad as a silken Disraeli stovepipe hat
hiding a gypsum-white rabbit.

She once told me – the malt talking –
I wasn't her first born boy;
there had been seminal drafts.

She said being pregnant
was like spinning a bone-china plate
on the thinnest stick inside you –

breakages were bound to occur.
It was a question of which piece
could drop intact and roll around

on a hardwood floor, its rim ringing
with cries. My sister is a wild firing,
an artisan's multi-coloured plate

still atwirl. I am a white canteen
saucer, ready to be tanned with tea-
slops. A cupped palm for spillage.

Weekend Break

At the coast they stayed in a B&B
furnished with bailiff's swag, auction-
bought driftwood, intestate jetsam.

They woke to the snigger of gulls
in the looms, faded amateur water
colours often found in hospices.

He had never tasted oysters before,
more interested in the opal faience
of the shells, the selfish inward lustre.

She had eaten them a few times,
salty jouissance, the hope of a pearl,
the taste of drowning, of sea-hockle.

A smasher of china, unraveller of silks,
the nurse's Dettol hands weeded out
the root that had grown in her dark.

Marion McCready

© Marion McCready

Marion McCready was born on the Isle of Lewis and lives in Argyll. Her poetry pamphlet collection, *Vintage Sea*, was published by Calder Wood Press in 2011. She won a Scottish Book Trust New Writers Award in 2013 and won the Melita Hume Poetry Prize in the same year. Her first full-length collection is *Tree Language* (Eyewear Publishing, 2014).

Wild Poppies

And how do you survive? Your long-throat,
your red-rag-to-a-bull head?

You rise heavy in the night, stars drinking
from your poppy neck.

Your henna silks serenade me
under the breadth of the Pyrenees.

You move like an opera,
open like sea anemones.

You are earth's first blood.
How the birds love you.

I envy your lipstick dress.
You are urgent as airmail, animal-red,

Ash Wednesday crosses tattooed on your head.
Your butterfly breath

releases your scents, your secrets,
bees blackening your mouth

as your dirty red laundry
all hangs out.

The Unintelligible Conversation of Unpicked Rhubarb

Silver rain flies through tumbleweed trees.
Black-eyed brambles are knocking at the door.
The babies lie, three, on the dining room floor.
One named Forty and one named Four.
And the other, face-down, is no more.

Daffodil horns

                        star-splayed
mouths from the yellow bellies
of starfish   flat and helpless
mouths   unshuttable   though mute
unstoppable   culled from our garden
these lampshade-and-bulb trespassers
periscope from the bottom of a foreign vase
though we listen   we do not hear
though we see   we do not understand
and the daffodils   they spread like cancer

Rachel McCrum

© Chris Scott

Originally from Donaghadee, Co Down, Northern Ireland, Rachel McCrum has lived in New Zealand, Belfast, Manchester, and is now based in Edinburgh. She studied English Literature and Language at Jesus College, Oxford. Her pamphlet *The Glassblower Dances* (Stewed Rhubarb Press, 2012) won the 2013 Callum Macdonald Award. Alongside poet Jenny Lindsay, she runs the Edinburgh spoken word and music cabaret Rally and Broad.

Broad

In a Belfast sweatbox
slurred and steaming
a country voice dove into my ear.

'Jaysus. You're a hefty one.'

I believe it was a compliment
he thought
he paid.

These shoulders are broad.
My mother was a farmer's daughter
with a voice that stretched
across three fields.

From her, I gained
blue eyes
child bearing hips
and feet planted family tree trunk
to the ground.

From her, I learned
that self indulgence is a dirty word.

That it is important
to get the potatoes on the table
for your brothers
before you write the application
for the university.

She did both.
The first in the family to live by words
rather than by her hands

and she suffered uncharacteristically quiet
I think, for this.
It can be hard to explain the weight of paper.

In the church hall, after my great grandmother's funeral,
they turn over my palms
as they clasp my forearms
to see if I have yet managed
an honest day's work.

I have only one callous to show them.
The indentation
between the knuckles
of the middle finger
of my right hand.

The
last
best
thing
my mother
gave to me.

Zippo Endings

The lighter you gave me as a parting shot broke
two days after you had peeled yourself from this town.
The wheel jammed like our
stilted final conversation
calloused up my thumbs
and guttered out.

A brass necked Zippo
fit smooth to the palm
like a significant pebble
from a trip to the ocean
we never quite made.

You should have handed me
something cheap
and plastic. Filched,
then lost, not quite finished
to the bottom of someone else's handbag.

Or, as I think I will not pick you up again,
let's give a savage flare to the linger of things.

Pretend you left
a book of charred matchends
on my empty bedside table
as you slid out the door.

The Glassblower Dances

The words first appeared on a lamppost
on a dirty road between a chip shop
and some tired Turkish Baths.

They nestled amongst fat careless splurges of paint
and the neon screams of *get tae fuck*
and *nae future*.

Reading the phrase, passersby smiled
briefly
and thought no more about it.

But the words tucked themselves
into the minds of the people
on the bus.

Two days later, the handwriting was seen again
on a wall along a cycle path
and beside the hospital for sick children
and in a cafe toilet
and down near where the ships no longer came.

And people began to repeat it to themselves
in the early morning on the streets.

The phrase swirled out.
It appeared on the back of schoolbooks
and on library desks.

It moved beyond the city

was seen written on a rock
on a beach full of leaving birds
and on a bench
beside a bus stop
in a small grey town.

It was seen carved down the curve of a mountain

the glassblower dances.

As the words swelled
people began to talk.
A feature was broadcast on the local news.

And some were curious
and searched for understanding
on YouTube

removed

but enough to understand
the rhythm that came through the feet
from earth to breath to arm
the flow of skill
the exhausted dogged passion
that was required for the alchemy of changing
dirt into something fluid, strong and beautiful.

The words grew.
And the City Council talked
of the cost of cleaning
but they could not calculate it accurately.

And well heeled sorts on a late night sofa
spoke of the shallowness of modern culture
and lamented the loss of the canon.

(But the thing about a scratch
is that you feel it
and sometimes it lets things in
and they incubate
and fester)

And some academics wrote a paper
on the sociocultural intertextual significance
of urban public expression

but it was rather long
and only read by eight people.

And linguists spoke of sibilants,
how they trace the brain with fingers of smoke.

And historians expounded on the history of glassmaking
how China, ignoring it until the Seventeenth Century,
invented fireworks instead of windows.

And the phrase didn't stop any wars
or bankers –
there were other words to try that job
and it was beyond this writer's ability
at this time.

But people smiled
and for a moment felt something in their chests had loosened
and wondered about things
that did not touch their lives.

And all this happened
because once upon a time
someone thought to write
upon a wall with joy
the glassblower dances.

McGuire

© Chris Scott

McGuire writes he is 'A thin Glaswegian man, touch giddy in the head, sometimes poet of mangled form and dirty prose, sporadic drummer, drunk grammarian, waffler, painter using crayons, lover, hater, learner, teacher, pedestrian, queer provocateur, wanderer, confronter of shadows, irritating whiner.' He has published a collection of poetry and short stories, *Riddle With Errors*, and released his first chapbook called *Everybody lie down and no one gets hurts* (Red Squirrel Press, 2013). His first full-length collection is *As I sit quietly, I begin to smell burning* (Red Squirrel Press, 2014).

Delta Phos b.

(Delta Phos b. is a protein in the brain associated with addiction.)

Digital harem eroding will power,
fucking with the frontal cortex.
Alone and voyeuristic, hermetically sealed
in the anonymity of webcam dark
confessional box, tomb of a hot bedroom.

O pornocopia. Schools of bodies
open before our helpless sight.
Endless novelty in new windows.
Playboy, what have you done to us?

Every candy on offer
buxom mistress dominatrix
double entry fist pumping
rim shot vanilla extract.

Shock horror schools of Lolitas, undressing.
Tadzios in tight fit Speedos,
with sunlit smooth caramel torso.
Housewives in loose lace, stroking
incomprehensible geological rocks.

Masturbating a miracle, glittering splashes
of jizm into innocent white handkerchiefs.
Lonely isolate men in solitary decade rooms
dreaming of ice cream Monroes.

Boys fapping athletic over heavenly body
imagery of airbrush illusion.
Mature Vixen toys with desire in dungeons
of pay-per-view vagina churches.

Instantaneous pederasts at the touch of a button.
Older female dominates cam-shy boy in Heaven.
Gerbil geek searches for ladyboys
with suicidal clouds of loathing hanging.
Octopus clitorises swallow the screen wide.

The mouse of the brain spins
on the reward wheel of its system;
every jerk-off cements a neural pathway.

Internet unconscious streamer
of every fleeing desire.
We huddle round your tabernacle
illuminations, seeking an answer
to the mystery of sexual identity.

Great unconscious shadow
of internet search engine.
Every dark thought googled
in secret vaults of shame.

We drink from you, endless,
fountain of perversion,
attached inescapably to wifi's connectivity.
What has been seen cannot be unseen.

Innocence molested
through the all-seeing eye,
exposed to every adult sweetie.

O poor human cycle of fixation.
All feeling fragmented to a pixelation.
Our better natures smothered by impulse.

Generations of young men
pump for the protein.
Delicate sensoriums
exposed to the cameras lens.
Touched too soon
by the network's eely finger.

What will become of simple affection
and neutral tonic of care,
when everybody is reduced
to a touch pad, sex pod, reaction?

Reducio Ad Absurdum

Shakespeare's more a performance poet
a throat poet, a fire and tongue type.
A poet of larynx, a diaphragmatic breathing poet
not a serious poet in gentleman's jacket.

I'm a page poet; a take-the-time-to-consider-
the-exact-length-and-breadth-of-the line poet.
I am an architect with form but never formulaic.
I am a master of design but never mastered by it.

Hughes's more a performance poet;
a wave-your-arms-gesticulate-wildly-and-know-it.
A show-it-all-and-throooooooow-it-at-you poet.
Not a serious poet who reads the classics and shows it.

I'm page poet, a literary allusions and allegorical conclusions poet.
A lay-subtle-structures-that-unravel-a-slow-burning-conundrum poet.
I take the time to create something so delicate a breath could break it,
yet it withstands that breath, and you cannot break it.

Sexton is more a performance poet; a shout-at-the-top-of-your-soul
    poet.
A rant-in-the-mirror, solipsistic, I-alone-exist-and-will-prove-it poet.
A should-have-been-an-actor-instead-but-never-knew-it poet.
I-wrote-this-on-the-loo-and-you-can-smell-it poet.

I'm a page poet with stable demeanour and quiet composure.
I build sturdy liners out of the thin matchsticks of words
that set sail quietly on calm waters across oceans of eyes.

Rimbaud is more a performance poet.
An of-the-internet-attention-deficit-quickly-type-it-with-no-edit poet.
A scribbler of slapdashery, a knee-jerk reactionary
bound to be burned as waste under the well-read eye of reality.

I'm a page poet. An on-the-crusade poet. Here to explode
the false dichotomy of page and perform-it, show-and-tell-it poet.
Let the words carry the weight we carry. Let tastes divide.
Quality lingers upon the shelf life longer than the debate will have it.

(In the jungle the soul's wild eyes glare white in the shadow.
The cauldron of the heart sounds like a warm drum.
We search continually for that which is comprehensible.)

The Glasgae Boys

Glasgay gender bending sex offending
all soft down The Merchant of Penis,
down Glasholegreen,
down The Gallowgay,
down SuckyMaHoleStreet,
down Tendergrove Park,
down the WestBenders.

Q: What do you get if you mix Green with Blue?
A: Turquoise.
Q: What do you get if you mix White and Red?
A: Pink.

O, the pink and turquoise boys.
Come roll yir bawz around way each other.
The boys in the pink and turquoise,
ma Son better not play for the other side.

Aggression in The Bar for Repressed
Homo-Erotic memories.
Knife Crime as metaphorical sodomy.

Affection is a laughing matter,
all feeling reduced to a wank
after a few pints over some blonde number
with her hair bleached right to the cerebral cortex.

Fitbawmen way daffodil hearts
drinking under the table their tender selves,
soaking in the pub, splashing in the shallows,
seeking carnal pleasure down the Clyde.

Gender bending sex offending.
Get that boy down the boxing ring,
we'll make a punch bag out of him yet!
(But have you seen his calf muscles?
Smooth as marble, long caramel brown,
tight as a taut rope.)

Poofs, man, who needs them?
– Bennets Shite Club
– Polo Nob jockeys
– The Glasgow Pink Pound.
O chasing after the pink pound
with a feather outstretched to tickle an arsehole.

My son could have danced
Billy Elliot down in London
but he hung himself from a penis
and tied his mother around his neck.
Rather he swung from a tree
than fir the other side.

Glasgow used to be a knife.
Glasgow used to be a gangland Disneyland.
Glasgow used to be an old man's pub.
Glasgow used to be a betting man's game.
Glasgow used to be the razor against the soft cheek.
Glasgow used to have a third world life span.
Glasgow used to belt her pupils red raw.
Glasgow used to drink her men to the graveyard.
Glasgow was all woodbine, bitter and bookies.
(Naw pal, that was just a Peter Mullan film.)
Glasgow is all cappuccinos and croissants.
Glasgow is all baguettes and pan au chocolat.

Just ask Billy Connolly. His Father molested him.
Poor Billy, aye. Wouldn't be half the man he was today
if he wasn't first robbed of half the child he could have been.

Glasgow – whit's yir agender?
Hetero-normative default setting,
none of this metro-sexual, rainbow
on the horizon, bisexual reality,
ying and yang,

      woman inside of the man
        inside of the woman
          inside of the man.

None of this hetero-flexible, omni-sexual,
bending a little, frying pan sexuality.
I'm a man's man but not a man's man for *'aw that.'*

Glasgow. We do not tend to it,
but watch it blacken like a burst eye,
blacken like a coal pit,
blacken like a dead flower.
We do not tend to feeling.
Centuries of shame, shadowing the city.

nick-e melville

© Anne Laure Coxam

nick-e melville makes found, visual and quasi-conceptual stuff. He was writer (not) in residence at HMP Edinburgh 2010-2011 and is currently doing a PhD in creative writing at Glasgow University.

from *Alert State Is Heightened*

ALERT STATE IS HEIGHTENED. This is a security announcement. The cuts and attacks upon the poor, low paid and vulnerable will continue. STEP UP I'm afraid I can't stand. I am unsure what I say or do. Business as usual. Old soldiers never die. They get younger   everyday. Their name liveth for evermore. Wash your hands of them. Hardship is being forced upon far too many. Community Life in action. Scotland's best visitor attraction. The healing properties of Scottish heather honey. Working for you. There have always been young people. We sacrificed our lives for Britain. Observe the IV tubing drip chamber. THE GLORIOUS DEAD. Let's sing! The traditional music which has never been changed. You have talents, we have options. RECRUITING NOW. Building a smarter future. Turn handle firmly to left then right. Keeping people safe. God Save The Queen. I am certain it is being considered. No smoking. Remember them. AHEAD ONLY. This bus is different. This train is for Edinburgh Waverley. Supporting our heroes. Talk to us. 'Marco Polo discovered Italy.' The lord lift up the light of his countenance upon you. A new dawn for Lotto. I can't watch. Gold loses its shine to shares for investors. Thank you for your unforgettable support. We do not have control over social security and benefits. Giving what we can, doing as much as we can. All texts are ultimately political. The words are maps. Provokes mild outrage. I do it in the stationery cupboard. It's so easy. Your communities. Your decision. A helping hand to let you live where you love. Life needs a great venue. The big night in. The benefit changes that have been brought in by the

Westminster government are causing undue hardship and misery. He who wants to live must work. An hour of darkness. Blossom this winter. Take an hour . . . save a day! Believe in magic & sparkle. Heading for the stars. Lights up nights out. Observe Flow Rate. These things are important. . . . you deserve it. House prices are out of reach for young people and families. Woodlands for sale. The Tory led government has cut the affordable homes budget by 60% and they are presiding over the lowest level of house building since the 1920s. The flowers of the forest are all withered away. We welcome you. Designed with families in mind. Making your home safer. Live well for Less. Meals served here. We care about here. Make your dream home a reality. Danger. Demolition in progress. Feel at home. Soil from battlefield to be brought to UK. Update your life. THE DEAD SHALL BE RAISED. We're going smart! Let's read.

cu ts[1]

LIBERAL

███████████████

tough choices needed to cut
millions
more have taken pay cuts
we will cut
██ completely
cut too soon
cuts on an objective
bear cuts
they need to cut
to cut class ██
to cut classes
We would cut the size
of the central department of children
prevention measures   Cut
cut the budgets of the rest

███████

cuts to ███
its target to cut child poverty
Cut rail charges
a real-terms cut
effectively to cut crime
transport and cut
what works to cut crime
of a fair society and the best way to cut
██ the traveller and cut
Cut rail fares
a real-terms cut
to private cars, and cut
cut back central government
by reforms that cut
through spending cuts
██ could not be found
make net cuts

---

1 all CU TS from the conservative, labour and liberal democrat manifestos, in order as they appeared

fenced from cuts
place cuts which could be realised
put into place cuts
the remaining cuts
scheme Cut
██ education
civil service bonuses Cut
sector Cut ████
government Cut
on bank profits Cut
top brass Cut
████████

LABOUR

risk by reckless cuts
people's savings, cut
We will not cut
cuts to lower priority
identified in cuts to lower priority
with cuts this year
and cuts to lower priority
should be cut immediately
in the future. To cut
cuts in lower-priority areas
will be cut by more than
two-thirds
cut them. And we have made our choice
cut at ten months
cut. More people
not cut. As family
—not cut—the Child
would cut police
elsewhere: continuing to cut
technology to cut crime

the taxpayer has been cut
by half
an easy target for cuts
████████ will be cut
back

130

and cuts to lower priority
█████ cut

CONSERVATIVE

government will take action now
to cut
So we will cut
include cuts

cut government contributions to Child
cut Ministers'
we will cut
Cut government
take action to cut
act immediately to cut
to cut a net
other countries have cut

boost employment. Cut
we will cut the headline
people cut down
this would cut fuel
the world's future. We need
to cut

cuts and reorganisations
will be able to cut the cost
get a grip and cut
that leads to violence. We will cut
police teams to cut crime
—payment by results—to cut
funding. We will cut the cost
cut the number
and cut Ministers'
cut Ministers'
cut the perks
cut the unaccountable
government will cut
cut household █████
▌ 10 per cent cut

we will cut
producers to cut back on production
cut across energy, education, community cohesion,
health, technology, international development and the environment

cut the target for the trained
the state cut off text

In the future

We are all interested in the future,
For that is where you and I are going to spend the rest of our lives.
And remember my friend, future events such as these will affect you in the future.
You are interested in the unknown . . . the mysterious.
The unexplainable.
That is why you are here.

In the future
even the smallest business
will   be
        multinational

In the future
the food chain and   the supply chain
will merge

In the future
South-South trade
will be norm   not novelty

In the future   investors
will need to   be
explorers

In the future
we will   be
planting   cities

In the future
age will   be
no barrier to   ambition

In the future
we will all fly
organic

In the future
it will take   many imports
to   make an export

In the future
there will   be
no markets left
waiting to emerge

There's a new world
emerging   Be
part of it

Theresa Muñoz

© Gavin McCutcheon

Theresa Muñoz was born in Vancouver to Filipino parents and now makes her home in Edinburgh. She has been shortlisted for the Melita Hume Poetry Award and has been a prizewinner in the McClellan and Troubadour competitions. Her work has appeared in *Best Scottish Poems, Poetry Review* and *Canadian Literature* amongst other journals. She wrote her PhD thesis on the work of Tom Leonard at the University of Glasgow. She is the online editor for the *Scottish Review of Books* and a regular contributor to the *Herald's* book pages. She is the author of the pamphlet *Close* (HappenStance Press, 2012).

Be the first to like this

kicking pine cones down the street
climbing the backyard cherry tree
lying in new sheets
waking in darkness   waking to snow
how your chest thickens when you're scared
how your voice bubbles when you're pleased
be the first to like
view of wind turbines from the train
golden tint on a glass of wine
gliding on rollerblades by the sea
waking so warm   waking on the beach
how your eyes flood when you're tired
how you laugh when you're relieved
like bridges creeks Frisbees
silly cat videos and Instagram photos
like strolling with a friend
between folds of trees
and your heart rolls out a big pink wave
and your lips recall something sweet
like skiing and ice-skating
zip-lining above trees at seventy clicks
blood thudding in your ears
like every new experience because it was new
to you   pocketed in your memory
like the first time you fed the ducks
at Stanley Park
and they stormed like villagers
to your feet

Google Page Twenty

Poor Google page twenty adrift in the internet desert
nobody comes to click on you witness your existence barely I
in my third hour of searching for ice wines in the valleys
of British Columbia you are the product of selected words
wine / winter / BC and the frustrated insistence of return, return
every topic and / or search terms has a Google page twenty:
the straight-backed Ariel font, the calm blue letters
the delicate coded strings of jargon and the ever so polite
Did you mean? above the net of stories from around the world:
how in Germany one vintner mourns his unfrozen grapes
with a picture of farmers knelt in the snow beside their vines
and me in the study bleary-eyed at 3am GMT
unable to stop clicking, clicking where outside the long grass
shivers and I click alone but not as lonely as you.

Life in the UK

To take the settlement test, I have to know.
My name, my birthday, my coastal home town.

Desk clerk reads my navy passport.
'You're from Canada?
My brother lives in Quebec, he loves to ski.
Why do you want to live here?'

To take the settlement test, I have to wait.
With other nationalities
in this room of black chairs and cold air.
You can bring a book and a couple chats in Polish.
I envy their held hands, their thumbed notes.
They murmur NHS, Beveridge Report, Loch Lomond.

To take this test, I studied for days.
I know everything. I know the English Kings,
the dark coins of the Iron Age,
the rock steps of the Giant's Causeway.

I know how many jurors in Scotland's High court.
The age you can drive, the age you must stop.
What to do with a broken fridge.
Ladies, don't stay married if he hits you.
I can tell you the day the Concorde first flew.

To take the settlement test everyone has to pretend.
Beyond this room's glass panes,
& fearful, flickering lights
this information is relevant, useful to our lives.

Desk clerk is kind but pretends to be stern.
She gives us pink sheets to sign.
Wide screens flick their grey gaze.
And I feel tense but ready in my arms.

She wishes us luck but warns:
'Once you press start there's no turning back'.

Michael Pedersen

© Ryan McGoverne

Michael Pedersen is a poet, playwright and performer who has collaborated with musicians, filmmakers and artists across the UK. His chapbook, *Part-Truths*, was published by Koo Press in 2009 and went on to become a finalist for the Calum Macdonald Memorial Award. This was followed by *The Basic Algebra of Buttering Bread* (Windfall Books, 2010). Pedersen's first full-length collection was *Play With Me* (Polygon Books, 2013). He is co-founder of the literary night and record label Neu! Reekie!, lyricist for the band Jesus, Baby!, and has written short plays for the National Theatre of Scotland and Edinburgh Art Festival. Chosen as part of Canongate's 'Future Forty' list in 2013, Pedersen was recently the recipient of the John Mather Charitable Trust 'Rising Star' Award.

Jobseeker

On a June morning, sodden
and weepy, I came back
to the broo:

its accordion of tones
and teeth, the wild eyes
of hirsute residents.

Like a marsupial conceals
a cub, I cradle a book
of Armitage's poems,

weaving through words
as electronic Job Points
gesture like madmen –

a few clicks and they know *exactly* how much
trouble you're in.
Most of us pretend
we don't have to be
here, delivering a haughty hymn
of honeyed triumphs.

Midway through the poem
'Man with a Golf Ball Heart',
I'm accosted by Neil: his thinning

silver hair and evocative paunch
cast a hostile shadow.
Come right this way, Mr Pedersen.

We meet with a collective pinkness,
his tongue a ticking indicator,
my words skidding tyres

racing through every ailment
neither of us have. The day
had been a diagram, until:

Is there anyone under your care
or who cares for you, on a full-time
or part-time basis?

At this point I crumble.
Neil has broken me.
Would I be here if there was?

X Marks the Spot

When we first met
you were too drunk to remember,
storing me (my looping arms,
cherry cheeks, trespassing
tongue) in your phone as lonely
Letter X. But I sort of dug

the anonymity – what's in a name
after all? As X, I'm Roman ten,
daunting, a variable – the nomad
of the alphabet; I'm raunchy
racy top-shelf triple X –
an emblem, not a word:

a superhero, of sorts.
The next day – by text –
my X is resurrected on your screen.
My message, too, will end
in X – a carnal bounty
for your pirate eyes.

Another meet, another kiss:
X morphs into Carla,
Carla, to an affectionate farrago:
Slugger, Muffley,
Toots, Moon-Pie.

We croon and cuddle,
bundling under your covers
and mine. Life was a sack
of strawberries, the future, jams
and spice. ALAS – I am
a SNOOP. Left alone I will

peruse your personals, burgle
your belongings; searching for
a bottle-opener
I stumble across your phone –
Come to MAMA. A professional
has an eye for it – whizzing past

amorous gunk, poetic prattle, like
a boxer skipping rope.
Let's get straight to the yolk:
this address book *has* grown
and where once was *my* X
there now is another!

A trophy letter, slumped
to a stamp of expiration,
no curlicues to mitigate its twin
crossing blades; X
the executioner; X a weapon of infallible symmetry.

Times New Roman
doesn't beat around the bush:
my years under your cover,
once absolute, suddenly
a shoddy leasehold tenure.
Nothing else for it,

time to take the plunge:
CALLING X – the ringing phone
cackles out with wry
tintinnabulation.
A silken, exotic voice
answers, with perfect

tongue and intonation
Good eeeevening
. . . you're through
to The Thai Palace.
Please order by inserting the number
of the dish you desire.

Ahhhhhh finest of fortunes,
pangs of a different stock.
You do love me!
Me, your estate for life,
love to the X
year – *pur autre vie*.

Laddie at Heart

At three-thirty I strode the buzzing
garden, entered an apricot door and stridently
announced an abduction. The illusive stranger:
he tried to take me – his leather bomber fastened
tight, puppies in the back of a beat-up Astra. Our

Bobbies on the job must have smelt a rat,
the story being nothing more than a sleazy replica
of the *Stranger Beware* tale they taught at school.
I made a statement, then marched a policeman
to a fictitious crime scene, barking boldly as I went.

By dropping in the odd nod of reverence –
I want to be a policeman when I grow up –
it panned out rather well. School signalled red alert,
Neighbourhood Watch was up in arms, and I
recounted details for tuckshop booty and lip kisses.

Conclusion: there's no better time for fame
than pre- the ego years. Silly to feign
a serious thing, but at ten – God knows what
I was thinking – it seemed a fair call. It's what I do
at twenty-five that gets my mother going.

Stav Poleg

© Stav Poleg

Stav Poleg's poetry has appeared in magazines such as *The Rialto*, *Magma*, *Poetry Wales* and *Gutter*. Her poem sequence on the goddess Athena was read at the Traverse Theatre. Her graphic novel shorts *Dear Penelope* (with artist Laura Gressani) has been recently acquired by the Scottish National Gallery of Modern Art.

I'm sending you a letter

Inside, I put a full-size blue guitar, a slice of sea (so you could shake it in a glass over the Mediterranean coast), a saxophone I borrowed from a local busker because I know you'd like her work, all my air-miles, so you could come and visit me, a crow, crushed ice, a glass of pink champagne, just open carefully, mid-August Edinburgh (a bunch of slightly boozed-up actors, a box of unpredicted rain). I marked: fragile, FRAGILE, all over it. Let me know when it lands or crashes into your hands.

Leftovers

For years I've been editing winter.
The rain, inaccurate. The sea,
acres of unwrapped water and nowhere
to find you,
even when I settled for finding you
in other people's coats
or move-abouts or late-night drunken
weather. Now I know
enough of winter to never
get it right. The season of failed forecasts,
recurring like a ritual,
as if seasons return only
to leave us
with the study of unsteadiness
and repetitions.

Sometimes I throw flat stones into the water,
to hear them hurt the sea.
On other days
I find the pathway to your winter, like in a kitchen,
open white cupboards and
close them, open and open the fridge.

Everything else

is fine.
We took the train today, pink champagne

and strawberries,
for an end-of-summer something

by the sea,
and there's the new patisserie

(jasmine macaroons that taste of green
and tea)

ten-minutes walk from where
we are.

I'm taking yoga twice a week
(Ashtanga Flow, I know!)

and have even tried some baking
(cherry skillet bread, upturned

tarte-tatin). Don't ask
me how I am.

Mornings are busy with hours.
Nights –

it's when I fall asleep (I never
fall asleep

these days before
it's morning), or watch

the moon moon into darkness,
the way it can,

until there's nothing there,
and for a day or two

the sky goes missing and missing-you
makes sense

(everything else is fine, we took the train
today) to me.

Tracey S. Rosenberg

© Chris Scott

Born in the United States, Tracey S. Rosenberg is the author of a historical novel, *The Girl in the Bunker* (Cargo Publishing, 2011), and two poetry pamphlets. She won the Mountaineering Council of Scotland 2013 poetry competition, and in the 2014 Brontë Society Creative Competition, her short story was selected as the winner by Dame Margaret Drabble. She's been awarded a New Writers Award from the Scottish Book Trust and two Creative Scotland grants. Active in the spoken word and literary festival scene, she's a member of Edinburgh-based spoken word groups Inky Fingers and Shore Poets, and she is Bookstalls Manager at the StAnza Poetry Festival.

Meeting a guy off the internet

Early October, so the infants are lolling around campus
making up excuses why they can't roll out of bed for tutorials –
their grandmother's died for the third time.
The wind taps my shoulder like that annoying friend
you can't get rid of because if you do, you'll have no one –
winter's coming, you're staring down the barrel of thirty
and your flat has no heat
and you do realise the only people who get laid less than you do
are monastic?

Five minutes to go. I bet he's late
if he even turns up at all. Am I in the right place?
Once, I saw two restaurants with near-identical names
on the same street. He never even said what he does.
Something something computers.
Maybe he's really a spy, or a pirate, or a Tory –
oh dear God no, please not a Tory.
If he's wearing a suit, I'll flee,
pretend I was just loitering here
and now I have to run for my bus.
He knows how to use a comma,
but does he have any social graces?
In those pictures he posted he's going a bit thin on top
and they were all taken in the pub.
In *different* pubs.

I could just go back to the library, get a head start on preparing next
    week's lecture,
and ignore any messages he sends asking why I stood him up –
but he's standing *me* up, so he'll never know anyway.

Why are these students so stupidly young?
Whoever let them out into the world?
I bet they're all having sex every night.

Photophobia

I fluster along the diagonal beach, I grab and cram,
stealing fragments until my box rattles with light.

Snarling bottle caps with their ridged silver teeth.
Twisted gum wrappers, those hostile shells of foil.
The white diamond-laced feathers, and the dazzling sea glass
I scrabble from the sand before it slices my sight.

They glow in confinement
like a magpie's trinkets
like a miser's seawashed stones
closed within a casket,
a cardboard box that once held summer sandals.

I stumble down this seamy beach, all bias and shifting lines.
I scrape the shining blots.

When this beach is blank I stare straight on.
Pure flat sand. Pure sight.

Cancer villanelle

Needles plunge. Consultants come and go.
Today, leukocytes are easy to locate;
tomorrow, next year, they may sink below.

Taxol drags at her heart. The drip, so slow,
eases on, flowing down her hand's tight veins
as needles plunge and consultants come and go.

The nurses praise her husband's constancy, though
he's uneasy, each treatment – can he sustain
her, tomorrow or next year, if she sinks below?

The ward's fish flit through a new tank, even though
the fatigued walls sag with the same diseased paint.
Needles plunge. Consultants come and go.

She still submerges, cold, forlorn. She knows
he'll ease her to a surface of hours, days,
tomorrow. Next year, she might sink below.

Bloods, infections, bruises, vomit, soothing low
tones, fish rising in an easy ballet:
tomorrow, next year, all these could sink below
the needle's plunge. Consultants come and go.

Charlotte Runcie

© Charlotte Runcie

Charlotte Runcie is a former Foyle Young Poet of the Year and winner of the Christopher Tower Poetry Prize, and has a pamphlet, *seventeen horse skeletons* (tall-lighthouse, 2010). She has been published in magazines including *Magma*, *FuseLit*, *Read This* and *The Dial*, and is former editor of the *Pomegranate poetry* e-zine. In 2011 she graduated from Cambridge University with a First in English Literature and has appeared in the *Salt Book of Younger Poets*.

Staying In

I watch the city shrug its clothes back on.
An appaloosa spatter gathers scent
that hits the brain the way it hits a lawn:
it quenches, hard as mint. I think it meant
to come inside, but only leaves a note
in droplets on the door; at Hogmanay
it settles in the lungs and in the throat
and whispers too a hush of seaside spray
that sweeps below the ribs and keeps its snow
flakes back from hopeful tongues. I'm breathing when
the rainsmell pours my throat a dram, and so
I open up the window wider, stand again
here in our cloud and wincing, hats and boots,
a pearlish weeping reaching for the roots.

Lothian Road, Saturday Night

'hi we danced . . . i left, u got ur bag
sorry i didnt speak outside my mate was going fighting

me blonde hair

u black top'

– a Missed Connections listing on gumtree.com

Outside rain flared the sparks that dripped
from hogmanay rockets lit over us,
scattered in haar that reached across
to sob on seven shoulders.

Cold winced around. Your shirt disintegrated,
beer-transparent laced with air.

We could have stayed until the gun,
but you hungered for the heat
of a connecting punch.

I got my bag. You gone,
I walked among the stone
shocked wet as if you'd smacked it,

the tenements crackling with paint spot lights
dragged into stars by a drunk eye's toothpick.

Pope, Telescope

He smoothes its hands over its hips
and pulls its eye to rest against his own,
zooms into the dark to study fireflakes
strung up and blizzarding
across the dome of atmosphere.
Psalms and intercessions drift
in universal rafters, with Sunday smoke
from mouths, and lungs
broadcasting into black.

As he focuses the glass into the distance,
it doesn't seem to matter if
the star above the stable
was really only Jupiter,
bending closer just to see the fuss;

he means to keep an eye out for
his echoes bouncing off the asteroids,
in case an eardrum reaches up to catch
and beats a sacred cadence back.

Each night he sieves the cosmos through his sinuses
and scans the skies for codes, or explanations –
come morning, as the sun brights out for the blueprint
he swings a fiery meteor
to wash the earth in outer space.

Sarah Stewart

© Sarah Stewart

Hailing from Stonehaven, Sarah Stewart is an author, editor and director of The Lighthouse Literary Consultancy. Previously, she spent ten years as a journalist and maga-zine editor, writing for a wide range of publications, from *The Guardian* to *Mizz* magazine. Her poetry has appeared in *Anon, Mslexia, New Writing Dundee, The Pickled Body* and *The Scotsman*, and her first novel will be published by Stripes in 2015.

This is a true story

I would not marry into that house.
I couldn't condemn
my unconceived children

to their strange bloodline:
oddly shaped ears, a mad uncle,
small boys packed off to Eton,

and an imperious matriarch
reigning over the tea-table.
God, the mother loved to bake.

I was suspicious of her flirtation
with domesticity, seeing as
they had *staff*, but she was a pro

with the first incision,
opening up Victoria sponge
like a neurosurgeon,

and she'd wave that knife in the air,
if she disliked the conversation.
I marvelled at their gift

for turning near-miss into legend:
He almost rowed for Oxford, you know!
Giles practically climbed Everest in '92!

Years later, I found a photo of us,
frozen for the camera,
at a table covered with sugar.

I'd told the story to so many –
this crazy rich family! –
that I could barely recall

how much of it was theirs,
and how much mine. I confess,
matriarch held no scalpel

in the shot; the light was kind,
the cakes appeared delicious,
and all their ears looked fine.

Records

You were cool enough to own vinyl –
black stacks of tightly sleeved voodoo
shelved in artless disarray,
like anyone *really* leaves
the Velvet Underground out,
or that spine-cracked orange
Joseph Conrad, or a pile of coins
from some distant terrain.

If I'd eased open a drawer,
it might have held dental notes
for the brace you used to wear;
Scout badges; old school reports
or crumpled porn, but I didn't look –
and this way, we both slept.

MRI

In posh hospitals you get headphones, music
to dull the noise, but I told myself I'd *think*
my way through Dylan's second album.

The nurse murmured, "When you're in,
don't open your eyes", so of course
the first thing I did

was open my eyes. My skull
encased in plastic, a band of white
two inches above my stuttering eyelids.

Bob whined and crooned
his way through *Blowin' In the Wind*
as I floated upwards and into

Girl From the North Country
A Hard Rain's Gonna Fall and
Don't Think Twice, It's All Right.

Ross Sutherland

© James Lyndsay

Ross Sutherland was born in Edinburgh. He began performing poetry aged 17, as support for punk-poet John Cooper Clarke. His first collection, *Things To Do Before You Leave Town* (Penned in the Margins, 2009), was followed by a second *Emergency Window* (Penned in the Margins, 2012). Along with Luke Wright, Sutherland is one of the founder members of performance poetry collective *Aisle16*. A former lecturer in electronic literature and a self-confessed video game geek, he has completed a thesis on computer-generated poetry and writes univocalisms – poems written using only one vowel.

Richard Branson

My love, I feel like this print of Rothko.
I am small and glassy and I want to impress you,
even if it means murdering one of your work colleagues.

You think if you stare long enough at your noodles
you'll see the combination to the safe.
I don't have the heart to tell you the truth.

Even the elephant on the 20 Rand note
you gave me for good luck back in 2009
will end up spent in the end.

You adjust my tie and I grow a little older.

On cold hungover days, the white sun follows us
through Jesus Green to the Carphone Warehouse.

Shrek watches from the electrical shop across the street;
seven Shreks, running in parallel across a burning rope bridge.
It's impossible to root for any of them.

A millionaire's hairstyle
is trapped in the era that they first made their money.

The air turns green above the poles of the Earth.

555

Whenever a character on late night TV
watches some late night TV of their own
the only thing that ever seems to be
on the box is metaphor   the gang member
watching jackals on Discovery   the drug addict
glued to the end of White Christmas
the elder statesman who stays up long enough
to see the dead return from their graves   holy shit
this network knows its demographic
Queer Pets Attack Scotsmen returns next week
but coming up next on the metaphor channel
the closest thing you'll get to a satisfactory answer
when you follow the trail of x-radiation
from your bedroom back to the small of the lounge
and ask him what the fuck he's watching
as he turns to you in his snow-drift shirt with
the pepperoni print   eyes like Acme anvils
nothing in his head but a triple-five number
the dialing code we reserved for fiction
like a dick   drawn onto his cheek   in his sleep

Infinite Lives

I have helmed enough spaceships in my time
to understand a lounge in three dimensions.
My mind can pilot a lightweight craft through
the hazards of your mantelpiece. I can hide
in the nebula of your grandmother's curtains,
sky-dock on the lampshade. A Yorkie Easter egg
crumbles in my hands like the last words of
the Death Star. Burner of a billion ships,
I hold my head high under the glittering skies
of French campsites, return to find my parents
playing dominos by lamplight, reconstructing
the car dashboard, over and over, all of us
in preparation for some great crash yet to come:
the one I pray for every time we drive to Dixons,
the car whipping round, my body falling out the door,
like, *laters!* Head slipping across the intersection
like a foamy beer thrown along a bar. I used to watch
those bartenders and think that they were fakers.
But now I have watched the outtakes and OK I finally get it.

Samuel Tongue

© Kate V. Robertson

Samuel Tongue was born in Bath and grew up on a pig farm in South Wales. After completing an English degree and a Masters in Creative Writing at Exeter University, he ventured briefly into ministerial training for the Anglican Church in Wales. He has published poems in numerous anthologies and magazines including *Magma, Gutter* and *The List.* He won the Callan Gordon Award as part of the Scottish Book Trust's New Writers Awards (2013 / 14). His collaborations include work with Edinburgh Printmakers, cosmologists, electroacoustic composers, and particle physicists. A poem entitled 'The Laws of the Game' was published as part of the 2014 Commonwealth Games celebrations. He is poetry editor at the *Glasgow Review of Books.*

Oak Branch and Tree Warbler
After Shotei Hiroaki

Tiny bird perilous on pencil thin branch,
sure as she can be in this floating world.
Hard acorns drop into the still loch.
Even atoms are mostly absence,
electrons circling like birds
never coming in to roost.

Why I was so bad at clay-pigeon shooting

It was cold. It was raining. I was tired.
I cried 'Pull!' and tightened, tried to follow the whirring discus
to its apex, the point at which it would pause and begin its fall;
my eye filled with dark mountain,
the grey curve of two heron
sweeping back along the silver loch,
and the shotgun was an extension
of my ability to crush the world
in gunpowder and brass, and the recoil
went deeper than the soft socket of my shoulder.

On a carrier pigeon found dead in a chimney

Time has done its dissections, spread
the jigsaw on the kitchen table;

some wing bones – hollow radius and carpus,
a fretwork of struts and trusses –

interlocking ribs around an unsnapped wishbone;
a dirty claw, an empty skull, chalky with age,

and a tiny red capsule concealing
a cigarette-paper of code:

```
KLDTS    FQIRU
AOAKN    JRZCQ
```

pencilled clues to the pigeon's lost brains –
how it was tuned to the earth's magnetic field,

its beak a fixed compass point,
or an unmetalled sextant,

charting the gunfire, rising Verey lights,
the parachute flares; how it sensed sparrowhawks banking

like Messerschmitts, coming up fast;
how it dropped like a stone,

smashing heavy into the treetops,
shaking loose the coordinates of home.

Ryan Van Winkle

© Ericka Duffy

Born in New Haven, Connecticut, Ryan Van Winkle is a poet, live artist, podcaster and critic living in Edinburgh. He is currently Edinburgh City Libraries' Poet-in-Residence. He was awarded a Robert Louis Stevenson fellowship in 2012 and was listed as part of Canongate's 'Future Forty' in 2013. His first collection, *Tomorrow, We Will Live Here* (Salt, 2010) won the Crashaw Prize and his poetry / theatre experiment 'Red, Like Our Room Used to Feel' was one of the top ten best-rated shows at the Edinburgh Fringe Festival in 2012. He is also the host and co-producer of the arts podcast The Multi-Coloured Culture Laser and the poetry podcast for the Scottish Poetry Library. Find his website at www.ryanvanwinkle.com.

Gerontocracy

I never put my foot down or even tried
to govern and I never pushed a boat out
or offered straw for a poll and my mother
sometimes screamed so loud our neighbours
pretended to water their lawns and my father
would drink so much he'd lose his hearing –
my old man with his channels on yell
and my mother shouting it down.
That was our government and still
I do not think government is evil

or that conspiracy is anything but silence.
Maybe you and I needed bills
like old boys on capitol hill, maybe
we needed debate, gavel bangs, and lashings
of a whip. But I couldn't call that government
to order because all I'd ever learned
of government was from Father's hand
across Mom's face and all I ever learned
of talking was from the tv so loud
it spun out everything honest

so I could not tell what was puppet
and what was shadow. So, when my mother
finally took to the lawn and threw her eyes
at her own home I think I understood
the single government of my father
like the night you came home drunk,
your feet wet from the walk and I spied
your new congress and wished
my own government wasn't owned
by the same old ghosts of old men
who only listened to their lawns,
cashed their checks and kept up
the monosyllabic megaphone
till the garage door opened, the engine
turned and we were left with noise

and the cold majority
of silence below noise.

Under Hotel Sheets

And the mother with scarlet baby biting
and the trucker with the bullet whore, crying

though he'd like to do more. And the newlyweds
too poor to go too far – but still he brings crimson,

and the nurse escapes, blots her mascara
on paper sheets which dry an ink spill,

and the farmer sweats the night
and goes back to grass the next day,

and the male too scared to shit,
waits for the balloons to break.

And only yesterday I was told
of my grandmother below hospice sheets,

and there's angel dust in skeletal lamp light,
brown, moth-size burns left on the shade.

And someone looked out this window,
and someone spilled wine for the floor

and you have to tell yourself without fear
where this goes, and what we leave,

what remains whenever
we are a little bit gone. And how many

others have had this bed and done
what I've done – come in a hand

beneath whispering sheets,
wiped their ghosts on white before sleep?

Our Door, after a Turbulence

I am always depressed
    after hard turbulence,
    the craft shaking like paper

finding myself alive
    and not at my funeral
    with no one looking
    for my little bones,
    my diaries of marrow.

See, I loved you always
    and always I dream
    that you will look for me,
    find a sign in my bones,
    craft a sternum pendant.

And I am surprised
    as them when we land
    and our world continues
    with a stamp and a taxi
    till I am at our door,
    sucking my breath
    before turning the key.

Samantha Walton

© Samantha Walton

Samantha Walton has published three chapbooks: *trist-anundisolde* (Arthur Shilling Press, 2010), *City Break Weekend Songs* (Critical Documents, 2011) and *Amaranth, Unstitched* (Punch Press, 2013). In 2011 she co-organised ConVersify, a three-day poetry conference and festival at the University of Edinburgh and the Scottish Poetry Library. She completed a PhD at the University of Edinburgh in 2013, specialising in detective fiction, psychology and law, and she now lectures in English Literature at Bath Spa University. During 2013, she co-organised the Syndicate poetry series in Inspace, Edinburgh with Lila Matsumoto, Jow Walton, and New Media Scotland.

be HAPPINESS: now

i, if you'll let me, have forgotten your name
helen, mark, steve, your names are the carnivalesque
prelude to forgiveness,
a forum made of tin foil, modroc & lace for indifference
my attempt to construct a convincing reality out of people
i never really believed in
memory is a patched-up and slumping mattress
a sticky dress you borrowed out of politeness
a digression – when friends are people you wouldn't recognise on tv
because, i never asked you to be my friend
& no one can disappear completely
terror isn't something you can just pop in the sea
i want to ask my spring greens the story of their lives
riot, now, reproduce, now
rent a mountain with your last dime
& dance to the natural rhythms that i show you while i take my
photo
in which soil did your populace grow, little flower?
whose little mind has my mind conquered?
be HAPPINESS: now
be not estranged
cut up the strangler with your notice
and slice abuse from the minds of bereaved – make a scarf
for the eyes of the saturated & laugh off infidelity
section the solicitors & squat in the bureau of national statistics
file sighs &
fold your hands into mine
we'll change the meaning of unclean
for my hostility read nostalgia, for bouts of silence read I LOVE
YOU
if i had an identity, it would be in spasms
with your large voice & your benevolence
please teach me mindfulness like a bad science

Move away, never come back

we live in a wee cottage
are charged tuna for rent
stapling milk to bread and through the postal vote i say
we should save ink and spend Thursday finding flowers
according to my stats there's samphire at Fort William
scratching the shore like deep fat, the row that will never erupt,
the significant ideological shift that is occurring right now
but which i just don't, like, feel in my guts

This messy poem called FEELINGS

take any product
from the next room
scanning sentiment
& the heart of the city is
stacking in photocopiers
all you say of love I can get from
posters, devices
everything's subtle in a spit of graffiti
doubleparked out of recklessness & backed into
a dripfed drama
buttonless, gums blazing &
car sick, cash strapped & full of
vim. let's churn out a classic
come with me
take this product [& then some]
my lovely gris gris
won't you
have a hold of my lovely gris gris
    At market, my clean canvas wedges named *Timeless* sink
lace deep in Bohemian patience. I have renamed my sandals
Harlem Renaissance and crash down the avenue with its
wretched overflow, catching the eyes of the traders whom I dare to love
my ankles a testament to my good faith in them, us all
my community a promise I make with my purse
We can't speak for the world but we can ensure
we drown evenly: the roads the sun made;
the beach under the beach still processing its feelings.
We are all about the present – and we know it's getting passé
writing poems about Tescos, but as
        we are the fluff of trade
we know when to hold our breath
when to learn ways to be pacific, to watch the
movement of bodies just glad to be alive as the earth
folds, boxes and packs itself away
    I can't love under these conditions, meet me

somewhere out of town, get away from this
we'll read each other long and impossibly sad love poems
I model! I cut myself into my perfect husk and I die by my own
violence! the one I love asks me how my fingers
felt to the touch : to the touch of asphalt? : I am crouching
in her corner and being watched to enliven and lionise her
I hope she finds the inside of my heart is beautiful Formica

Nuala Watt

© Liz Munro

Nuala Watt was born and lives in Glasgow. She has an M.Litt in Creative Writing from the University of St Andrews. She is currently studying for a PhD on the role of partial sight in poetic composition at the University of Glasgow. In 2009-10 she was a member of the Clydebuilt mentoring scheme run by St Mungo's Mirrorball. She is a member of several Glasgow poetry groups and is active in the local poetry scene. Her poems have appeared in *Magma* and *Gutter*, as well as on BBC Radio.

Eye Test

"Quite good at moon, especially when it's full,"
I boast by text message, as though the moon's
a new phase in my history.
My friend has asked if I can see its shape
in the bright dusk. Which image does she want?
A lump of rock? A leaping lunar hare?
Face? Crescent? A leech lifting
light from the sun? I can't say "Zilch"
or that the only Moon I'm certain of
is a sort of Braille, and as I can't read
the sky at night, the moon is a guessed space
where I am free to put whatever.
I suppose I could blame the weather
but I still hope to see the official moon
above rush hour. I respond
as though to an ophthalmologist
with a box of silver lenses,
whose job it is to clarify my dark
and gauge the exact colour of my blackness.

Dialogue on the Dark

and could be the freedom of shapes from their cumbersome names.

Allow me my vision at ease.

Eye quietness.

Grievously metaphored sign of a slandered season;
all-purpose hex: assassin; foxes' time.
I wish I could appoint a lawyer for winter.

Let there be an amnesty.
Sit. Watch deep blues approach.
Walk. Loiter in low light as though your family were blackened trees.

Untitled

I once heard a river as a car,
hovered on a kerb to let the breeze pass.

Traffic is each walker's indrawn breath.
Cyclists make the darkness move nonstop.

I walk on my ears,
the road changing shape as I eavesdrop.

J.L. Williams

© J.L. Williams

J.L. Williams was born in New Jersey and studied at
Wellesley College and on the MLitt in Creative Writing
at the University of Glasgow. She moved to Edinburgh in
2001. She is particularly interested in cross-form work and
has collaborated with artists, musicians and filmmakers.
She was awarded an Edwin Morgan Travel Bursary from
the Scottish Arts Trust and in September 2009 she jour-
neyed to the Aeolian Isles to write a collection inspired
by Ovid's *Metamorphoses*, *Condition of Fire* (Shearsman
Books, 2011). Her second collection, *Locust and Marlin*
(Shearsman, 2014), explores the idea of home and where
we come from. Williams performs in the band Opul and is
Programme Manager at the Scottish Poetry Library.

Waltzer

See, from the hot air balloon,
floating like a wish in the blue sky,
how the battlefield is an ocean;
the meat of evolution
churned into a vast, ululating pool.

What rises is the skeleton of a man.

It is your bones, your doppelgänger –
your true self.

See how it waltzes in blood,
bites through the air as if air was fine-milled bread,
waves – you did not think it could see you but it can,
and as your eyes meet its holes,
you exchange places.

You stare up at the balloon.
You feel the red wind pass through you.
You breathe out steam.

Something falls from the sky.
What is it? You can almost make it out,
you can almost remember . . . that face.

Because You Are

You do not have to feel alone.
The trees will open their barks for you
and invite you into their heart.

There you become the substance of wood
ageing in circles and never suffering fear
of season's end, for trees
diurnal revolution – passing –
is triumphant and commensurate with change.

Enter the trees with your centre first
and your bones will follow
in harmony with the way of all things.

All Water

Been thinking a lot about gills,
how this flesh fringe can take in

water and air, how you can
catch a fish by tickling it

under its belly wearing silk
stockings on your hands.

How you can hold a fish
gently in the current's stream,

revive it
as if it were a lover

needing stroking, needing
the brush of lips over glazed skin.

What is it we do
when we take a fish or sip,

pluck an apple, kill a man
or beast? Are we stopping or continuing

an endless flow
whose movement is toward

home or origin, whatever that may be,
whatever that may be, home,

beginning, but what or where is this?
Was it a cloud that formed,

let the first pure diamond
drop from its wet womb? Was it

first the puddle evaporating
in billion years' young sun?

Is this why
everything keeps moving, why

the circle within the circle
within the circle turns?

Because there is no soil
worth dying for (it'll

have us soon enough). We
are mostly water and all water

is a thing that seeks a home but has no home
except that carved in earth by seeking.

Acknowledgements

Colin Waters would like to thank: Claire Rose for patience and editorial assistance; Alan Taylor for ideas; the photographers who took images of the poets (special thanks to Chris Scott); and the staff of the Scottish Poetry Library, particularly Robyn Marsack for advice on editing an anthology, and Jennifer Williams for suggestions. Thanks are due also to each of the publishers for granting permission to use the poetry. He would especially like to thank the poets who took part in the anthology, all of whom agreed quickly and with enthusiasm to allow their work to appear in *Be the First to Like This*.

The editor and publisher gratefully acknowledge permission to reprint copyright material in this book as follows:

PATRICIA ACE: 'Skye lines' and 'Diary in Old Age' from *Fabulous Beast* © Patricia Ace. Reprinted by kind permission of the author and Freight Books, 2013. 'The Clangers on Acid' © Patricia Ace, first published in *Gutter #4* (Freight, 2011). Reprinted by kind permission of the author.

JUANA ADCOCK: 'X', 'Pennies, or how I singlehandedly got us out of the crisis' and 'Pie Chart on the Global Distribution of Military Expenditure' © Juana Adcock. 'X' first appeared in *Gutter #1* (Freight, 2009). 'Pennies, or how I singlehandedly got us out of the crisis' first appeared in *Gutter #10* (Freight, 2014). Reprinted by kind permission of the author.

CLAIRE ASKEW: 'Bad Moon', 'Privilege' and 'Driving in Snow' © Claire Askew.

JANETTE AYACHI: 'Airports' from *Pauses at Zebra Crossings* © Janette Ayachi. Reprinted by kind permission of the author and Original Plus, 2012. 'Hiatus' from *A Choir of Ghosts* © Janette Ayachi. Reprinted by kind permission of the author and Calder Wood press, 2013. 'The Annabel Chong Documentary' © Janette Ayachi. 'The Annabel Chong Documentary' first appeared in *Gutter #4* (Freight, 2011). Reprinted by kind permission of the author.

KRYSTELLE BAMFORD: 'On the Death Mask of Dolly the Sheep', 'On Visiting the Sexual Health Clinic Before Work' and 'Two White-Tailed Lies: The Deer' © Krystelle Bamford. 'On the Death Mask of Dolly the Sheep' and 'On Visiting the Sexual Health Clinic Before Work' first appeared in *American Poetry Review*, Nov/Dec 2012. Reprinted by kind permission of the author.

JEREMY BEARDMORE: 'Waiting for them to go and have a coffee together', 'Song' and 'Vreakvolksonnet' © Jeremy Beardmore. A version of 'Song' appeared in *The Mays Anthology 2005* (Varsity Publications Ltd, 2005), ed. Robert McFarlane, Jonathan Beckman, and Arthur House. A version of 'Waiting for them to go and have coffee together' appeared in *Pilot #2* (2007), ed. Matt Chambers. Reprinted by kind permission of the author.

LORNA CALLERY: 'Pigeon with Warburtons' and 'Prelude to 24 hour alcohol licencing' © Lorna Callery. 'Pigeon with Warburtons' and 'Prelude to 24-Hour Alcohol Licencing' first published in *New Writing Scotland 30*, edited by Carl MacDougall and Zoë Strachan (Association for Scottish Literary Studies, 2012). 'A Piece of Rope' © Lorna Callery.

NIALL CAMPBELL: 'The Work', 'The Tear in the Sack' and 'North Atlantic Drift' from *Moontide* © Niall Campbell. Reprinted by kind permission of the author and Bloodaxe Books, 2014.

ANGELA CLELAND: 'The Suburbs', 'Cross' and 'Waiting for Connection' from *Room of Thieves* © Angela Cleland. Reprinted by kind permission of the author and Salt Publishing, 2013.

MIRIAM GAMBLE: 'On Fancying Film Stars', 'The New Michael' and 'Taking Corners' from *The Squirrels Are Dead* © Miriam Gamble. Reprinted by kind permission of the author and Bloodaxe Books, 2010.

ANDREW F. GILES: 'Soldier II', 'Henry Lord Darnley, syphilitic' and 'Going Garbo' © Andrew F. Giles. Reprinted by kind permission of the author. 'Soldier II' first published in *Gutter #5* (Freight, 2011). 'Henry Lord Darnley, syphilitic' first published in *Gutter #6* (Freight, 2012). 'Going Garbo' first published in *Magma #53* (2012).

HARRY GILES: 'Piercings' and 'Brave' © Harry Giles. Reprinted by kind permission of the author and Stewed Rhubarb Press, 2012. 'if you measure the distance between teeth they'll tell you' © Harry Giles. 'if you measure the distance between teeth they'll tell you' first published in *Clinic #3* (2013).

PIPPA GOLDSCHMIDT: 'From the unofficial history of the European Southern Observatory in Chile' and 'Physics for the Unwary' from *Where Rockets Burn Through: Contemporary Science Fiction Poems from the UK* © Pippa Goldschmidt. Reprinted by kind permission of the author and Penned in the Margins, 2013. 'The Ballad of the Immortal Gene' © Pippa Goldschmidt.

AIKO HARMAN: 'In Mobius' and 'How the Beasts Survive for So Long' from *Where Rockets Burn Through: Contemporary Science Fiction Poems from the UK* © Aiko Harman. Reprinted by kind permission of the author and Penned in the Margins, 2013. 'Immortal Jellyfish' © Aiko Harman.

COLIN HERD: 'the rebrand' from *Glovebox* © Colin Herd. Reprinted by kind permission of the author and Knives Forks and Spoons Press, 2014. 'cumbernauld', and 'eva longoria' from *like* © Colin Herd. Reprinted by kind permission of the author and Knives Forks and Spoons Press, 2011.

VICKI HUSBAND: 'On Being Observed', 'Jean's Theory of Everything' and 'What Do the Horses Think' © Vicki Husband. 'What Do the Horses Think' first published in *Northwords Now #23* (2013). 'Jean's Theory of Everything' first published in *Gutter #7* (Freight, 2012). 'On Being Observed' first published in *Smiths Knoll #49* (2012).

RUSSELL JONES: 'The Flat Opposite', 'Breathing Space' and 'After the Moons' © Russell Jones. 'The Flat Opposite' first published in *New Writing Scotland Volume 29*, edited by Alan Bissett and Carl MacDougall (Association for Scottish Literary Studies, 2011). 'After the Moons' from *Spaces of Their Own*. Reprinted by kind permission of the author and Stewed Rhubarb Press, 2013.

DOROTHY LAWRENSON: 'Viewmaster', 'The Nerja Caves' and 'Leaving Fife' © Dorothy Lawrenson. 'Viewmaster' and 'The Nerja Caves' first published in *Gutter #7* (Freight, 2012). 'Leaving Fife' first published in *Edinburgh Review #126* (2009). 'Viewmaster', 'The Nerja Caves' and 'Leaving Fife' appear in Dorothy Lawrenson's pamphlet *The Year* (Perjink Press).

WILLIAM LETFORD: 'Be prepared', 'A bad day' and 'Thurs hunners a burds oan the roofs' from *Bevel* © William Letford. Reprinted by kind permission of the author and Carcanet Press, 2012.

JENNY LINDSAY: 'Wisest is She' from *The Things You Leave Behind* © Jenny Lindsay. Reprinted by kind permission of the author and Red Squirrel, 2011. 'Edinburgh' from *The Eejit Pit* © Jenny Lindsay. Reprinted by kind permission of the author and Stewed Rhubarb Press, 2012. 'No Ball Games' © Jenny Lindsay.

MACGILLIVRAY: 'Ghost Dance', 'Photograph of Spotted Elk' and 'Lobo' from *The Last Wolf of Scotland* © MacGillivray. Reprinted by kind permission of the author and Pighog, 2013.

RICHIE MCCAFFERY: 'The Professional' and 'Spinning Plates' from *Spinning Plates* © Richie McCaffery. Reprinted by kind permission of the author and HappenStance Press, 2012. 'Weekend Break' first published in *New Writing Scotland 31*, edited by Carl MacDougall and Zoë Strachan (Association for Scottish Literary Studies, 2013).

MARION MCCREADY: 'Daffodil horns', 'Wild Poppies' and 'The Unintelligible Conversation of Rhubarb' from *Tree Language* © Marion McCready. Reprinted by kind permission of the author and Eyewear Publishing, 2014.

RACHEL MCCRUM: 'Broad', 'Zippo Endings', and 'The Glassblower Dances' from *The Glassblower Dances* © Rachel McCrum. Reprinted by kind permission of the author and Stewed Rhubarb Press, 2012.

MCGUIRE: 'Delta Phos b.', 'Reducio Ad Absurdum' and 'The Glasgae Boys' from *As I sit quietly, I begin to smell burning* © McGuire. Reprinted by kind permission of the author and Red Squirrel Press, 2014.

NICK-E MELVILLE: 'from *Alert State is Heightened*' © Nick-e Melville. Reprinted by kind permission of the author and sadpress, 2014. 'CU TS' and 'In the future' © Nick-e Melville.

THERESA MUÑOZ: 'Be the first to like this', 'Life in the UK' and 'Google Page 20' © Theresa Muñoz. 'Be the First to Like This' first published in *Gutter #8* (Freight, 2013).

MICHAEL PEDERSEN: 'Jobseeker', 'X Marks the Spot' and 'Laddie at Heart' from *Play With Me* © Michael Pedersen. Reprinted by kind permission of the author and Polygon, 2013.

STAV POLEG: 'Leftovers', 'Everything Else' and 'I'm sending you a letter'

© Stav Poleg. 'Leftovers' first published in *South Bank Poetry* #19 (2014). 'I'm sending you a letter' first published in *Gutter* #8 (Freight, 2013). Reprinted by kind permission of the author.

TRACEY S. ROSENBERG: 'Photophobia', 'Meeting a Guy off the Internet' and 'Cancer Villanelle' © Tracey S. Rosenberg. 'Photophobia' and 'Meeting a Guy off the Internet' from *Lipstick is Always a Plus*. Reprinted by kind permission of the author and Stewed Rhubarb Press. 'Cancer Villanelle' first published in *The Yale Journal for Humanities in Medicine* (2010). Reprinted by kind permission of the author.

CHARLOTTE RUNCIE: 'Pope, Telescope' © Charlotte Runcie. First published in *Seventeen Horse Skeletons*. Reprinted by kind permission of the author and the tall-lighthouse, 2009. 'Staying In' © Charlotte Runcie. First published in *The Salt Book of Younger Poets*, edited by Roddy Lumsden & Eloise Stonborough. Reprinted by kind permission of the author and Salt Publising, 2011. 'Lothian Road, Saturday Night' © Charlotte Runcie. First appeared in *Edinburgh Review* #135 (2012). Reproduced by permission of the author.

SARAH STEWART: 'Records', 'This Is a True Story' and 'MRI' © Sarah Stewart.

ROSS SUTHERLAND: '555', 'Richard Branson' and 'Infinite Lives' from *Emergency Window* © Ross Sutherland. Reprinted by kind permission of the author and Penned in the Margins, 2013.

SAMUEL TONGUE: 'Why I was so bad at clay-pigeon shooting'© Samuel Tongue. First published in *Magma* #55 (2013). Reprinted by kind permission of the author. 'Oak Branch and Tree Warbler' and 'On a carrier pigeon found dead in a chimney' © Samuel Tongue.

RYAN VAN WINKLE: 'Under Hotel Sheets' and 'Our Door, After a Turbulence' from *Tomorrow, We Will Live Here* © Ryan Van Winkle. Reprinted by kind permission of the author and Salt Publishing, 2010. 'Gerontocracy' © Ryan Van Winkle. First published in *Gutter* #5 (Freight, 2011). Reprinted by kind permission of the author.

SAMANTHA WALTON: 'Move away, never come back' from *City Break Weekend Songs* © Samantha Walton. Reprinted by kind permission of the author and Critical Documents, 2011. 'be HAPPINESS: now' and 'This messy poem called FEELINGS' © Samantha Walton.

NUALA WATT: 'Eye Test' First published in *Jacket2* (2012). Reprinted by kind permission of the author. 'Untitled' and 'Dialogue of the Dark' © Nuala Watt.

J.L. WILLIAMS: 'All Water', 'Waltzer' and 'Because You Are' from *Locust and Marlin*. © J.L. Williams. Reprinted by kind permission of the author and Shearsman Books, 2013.

Scottish Poetry Library
bringing people and poems together

From our beginnings with two members of staff and 300 books in a single room, we've grown to occupy award-winning purpose-built premises in the heart of Edinburgh's literary quarter. As well as offering free access to an unrivalled collection of over 45,000 items of Scottish and international poetry, we also house special collections. These include the Edwin Morgan Archive, a collection of national and international significance.

Visit us to discover:
- twentieth century and contemporary Scottish poetry
- poetry from around the world
- literary magazines and an extensive cuttings collection

- large pamphlet collection
- index of Scottish literary magazines
- CDs and tapes, braille and large print material
- bookshop stocking magazines and poetry titles

We provide a free reference service to the public, students, academic staff, schools, libraries, publishers and the media. We hold a large amount of critical material and can provide detailed bio-bibliographical and copyright information.

Find out more and listen to podcast interviews with poets at
www.scottishpoetrylibrary.org.uk
@ByLeavesWeLive and on **Facebook**
5 Crichton's Close, Canongate, Edinburgh EH8 8DT
T 0131 557 2876 E reception@spl.org.uk

SCOTTISH POETRY LIBRARY

By leaves we live